The Reason for the Season

Advent Devotionals

Plus Adult Coloring Pages

Written and Illustrated by

Brenda K. Hendricks

All Scripture quotations, unless otherwise indicated, are taken from the *Holy Bible, New International Version®*, NIV®. Copyright ©1973, 1978, 1984, 2011 by Biblica, Inc.™ Used by permission of Zondervan. All rights reserved worldwide. www.zondervan.com The "NIV" and "New International Version" are trademarks registered in the United States Patent and Trademark Office by Biblica, Inc.™

Scripture quotations marked (AMP) are taken from the Amplified Bible, Copyright © 1954, 1958, 1962, 1964, 1965, 1987 by The Lockman Foundation. Used by permission.

ISBN:0982658281
ISBN-13: 978-0-9826582-8-4

DEDICATION

This book is dedicated to my readers and fellow stress-relievers. I pray you enjoy the coloring pages as much as I enjoyed creating them for you and the devotions inspire, motivate, encourage, and cheer you as the day of our Lord's Advent approaches. Have a blessed season of gratitude.

CONTENTS

God's Gift   9

Joseph's Dilemma   13

What's in a Name?   17

God with Us   21

Angels We Have Seen   25

The Most Amazing Thing About Jesus   29

Much More to Christmas   33

Christmas Lists   37

A New Creation   41

Christmas Lights   45

Let's Decorate   49

The Reason for the Season   53

Con Sumer's Black Friday Blitz (part 1)   57

Con Sumer's Black Friday Blitz (part 2)   61

Reverence the King of Kings   65

A Personal Touch   69

What Did You Get for Christmas?   73

Christmas Communications   77

No Greater Love   81

Preparations   85

A Christmas Fast   89

Obedience   93

Expectations   97

Service for the King   101

Motivation   105

Christmas Ought to Be   109

Lacy Bohnes' Christmas Wish (part 1)   113

Lacy Bohnes' Christmas Wish (part 2)   117

Lacy Bohnes' Christmas Wish (part 3)   121

Lacy Bohnes' Christmas Wish (part 4)   125

Lacy Bohnes' Christmas Wish (part 5)   131

ACKNOWLEDGMENTS

Many thanks to my wonderful friends and critique partners. I couldn't have accomplished this without you. You have showered me with inspiration, blessed me with your time, and stretched my imagination with your suggestions.

Even more thanks to my sweet husband. You have put up with late nights, cold suppers (that you made), and my many moods. Yet, you continue to encourage my creativity.

Thanks to my daughters. You have listened to my ideas as well as my whining. You've given me reasons to continue and stories to write about. You always and forever empower my creativity.

Ultimate praise and thanks to my Lord and Savior, Jesus Christ who has blessed me so richly with these people. It is for You I write, draw, live, and breathe.

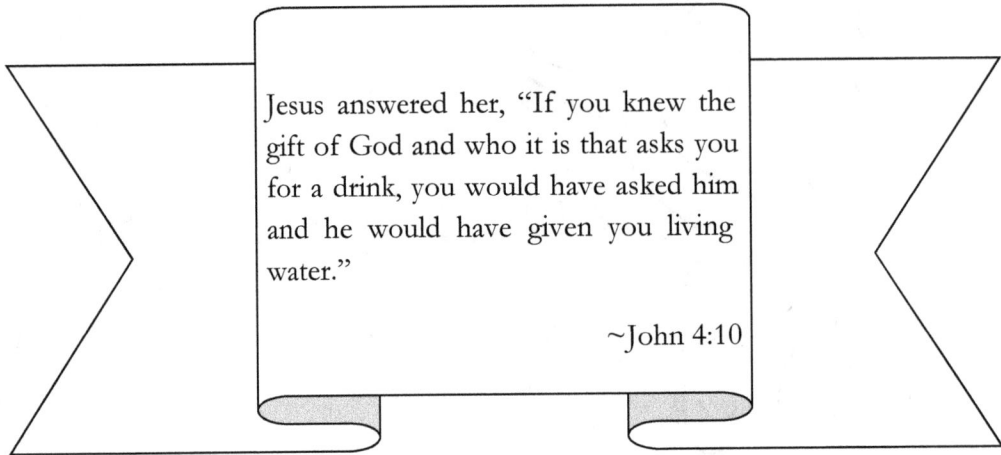

Jesus answered her, "If you knew the gift of God and who it is that asks you for a drink, you would have asked him and he would have given you living water."

~John 4:10

God's Gift

While speaking to the Samaritan woman at the well, Jesus refers to Himself as "the gift of God" or rather salvation, which comes through faith in Him. What a fitting thought to lead us into the Advent Season—Jesus Christ, God's gift to humanity.

On the eighth day after Jesus' birth, Mary and Joseph took Him to the temple to be circumcised and dedicated to God, as was the Jewish custom for the first-born son in those days. Luke 2:21-40 tells us about two elderly people who anticipated Jesus' first advent with great expectation.

The first mentioned, Simeon, a just and devout man, waited all his life to witness the "consolation of Israel." The Holy Spirit prompted the elderly man to visit the temple on the very day Mary and Joseph presented baby Jesus to the priest. While he held the infant, Simeon praised God with exhilaration as he proclaimed, "For my eyes have seen your salvation, which you have prepared in the sight of all nations a light for revelation to the Gentiles, and the glory of your people Israel" (Luke 2:30-32).

The second, Anna, an elderly widow who served God night and day with prayers and fastings, entered the temple at the time of Jesus' presentation and marveled at the sight of Him. She instantly gave thanks unto the Lord and told all who looked forward to the redemption in Jerusalem about Him.

These individuals maintained a close relationship with the Lord through prayer. They knew the Scriptures and believed that God would send a Redeemer to restore Jerusalem. When He came, they recognized Him and proclaimed the Messiah's birth without hesitation. They told everyone they had seen with their own eyes the "Gift of God" for the salvation of Israel and the light of the Gentiles. They concerned themselves with nothing more than the visitation they had anticipated for they knew their lives were complete in the knowledge of His advent.

Reflections

1. Think of new ways to praise Jesus. It's not all about singing Christmas carols or verbal praise. I like to paint. Last year, I created an a rt video and put it on YouTube as my "praise song" to my Redeemer. What special gift has He given you that you can return to Him in praise?

2. Tell others about Jesus' first advent. Remind those who already know, seek opportunities to tell someone who has never heard, and talk about Jesus' miraculous birth. We can do that through blogging, videos, Facebook and Twitter posts, and in church settings. But there's nothing like face-to-face conversations with neighbors and friends. Strike up a conversation about the true reason we celebrate.

3. Seek a clearer vision of Jesus Christ and cultivate a greater awareness of what it means to live our lives in expectation of the Second Advent of our Lord and Savior.

This Christmas, let's unwrap The Greatest Gift ever given and share Him with those around us.

Prayer

Heavenly Father, You have loved me with an everlasting love and have given me the most precious gift possible to prove Your love to me. Show me how to share Jesus Christ with those who need Him most this Christmas. In His name, I pray. Amen.

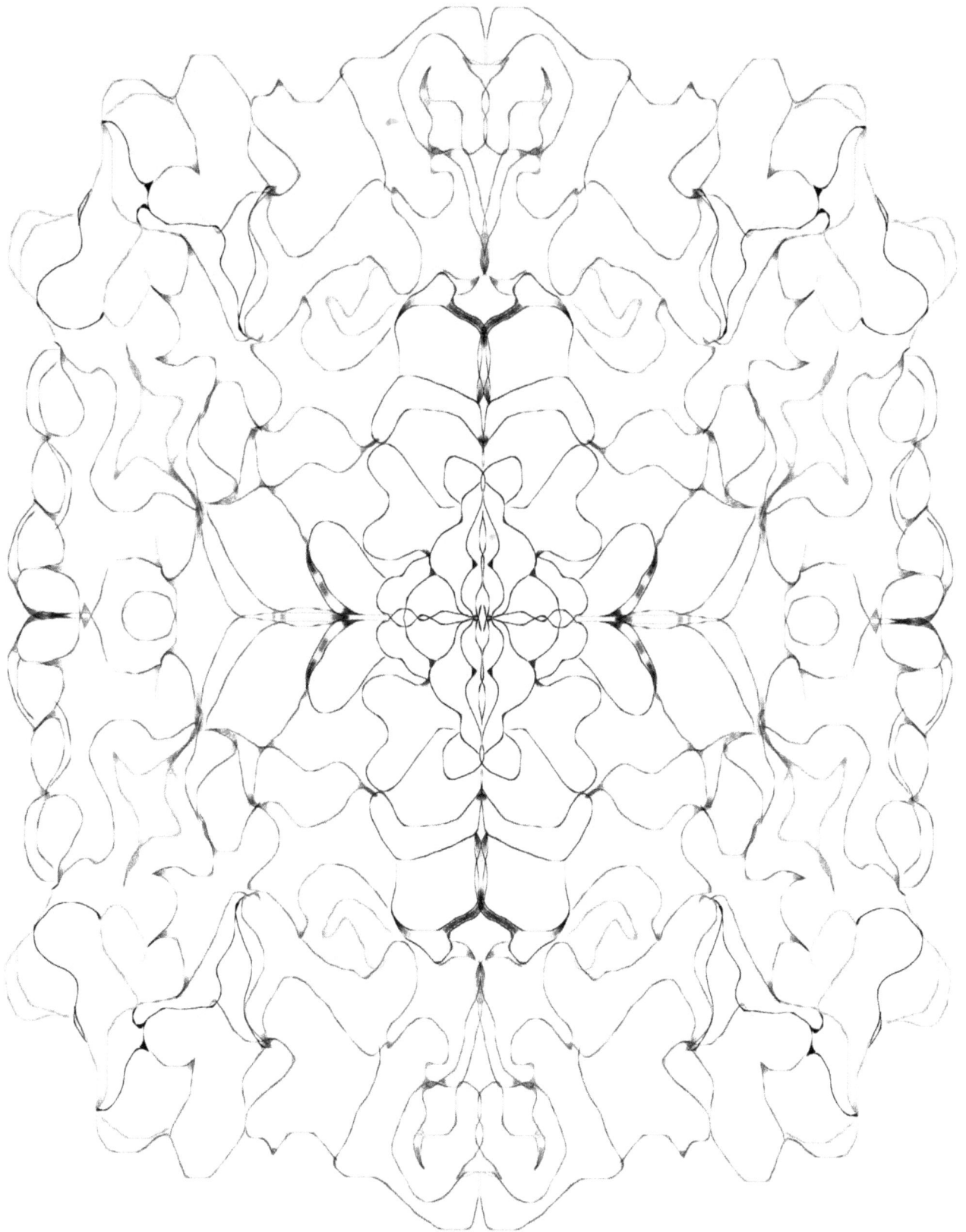

Mary was pledged to be married to Joseph, but before they came together, she was found to be pregnant through the Holy Spirit. Because Joseph her husband was faithful to the law, and yet did not want to expose her to public disgrace, he had in mind to divorce her quietly.

~Matthew 1:18-19

Joseph's Dilemma

As I study this portion of Scripture, I wonder how I would have responded had I been Joseph. Of course, it's difficult for me to put on a man's shoes. I reason like a woman.

I may have been so wounded by the news that I would 've wanted the full punishment for Mary afforded by the law. At least, that may have been my initial response before I had time to think through the situation.

Years ago,   a business associate betrayed me and tried to ruin my reputation. I trembled with frustration and fear that he might actually carry out his unwarranted threats. I wrestled with the thoughts of lawsuits for nights. I gave him plenty of time to reconsider his course before pursu ing the law. But he continued to press me until I finally, prayerfully called an attorney for help. I found out the law was on my side. I could have sued him for harassment. But I chose to drop the charges for the sake of peace and sanity. So maybe, if I had been cloaked in Joseph's situation, I would have tried to work out something other than public disgrace or death for Mary.

Here's what I've concluded about Joseph:

1. Mary's pregnancy left Joseph feeling betrayed by the one he loved. Being a faithful, law-abiding, righteous man, Joseph decided to apply mercy to the law, yet act within his legal rights to divorce her, by doing so quietly.
2. Although the Bible doesn't say so, Joseph must have prayed for an alternative. He loved God and sought His guidance in other matters, after all. Perhaps Joseph asked for a sign that he was doing the right thing in divorcing Mary.
3. To reassure and comfort Joseph, an angel appeared to him in a dream and reminded him of the prophecy about a virgin giving birth to the Messiah (Isaiah 7:14).
4. Joseph believed the Scriptures and looked forward to the Messiah, as did most Jews at that time. Joseph's faith was being tested. And he passed. He accepted the angel's explanation of Mary's pregnancy and took her to be his wife.

In regards to the Joseph scenario, I hope I'd have taken time to pray and seek God's will as Joseph did. He must have been in great distress. I mean God had to send an angel to convince him not to divorce Mary.

And how would I have reacted to an angel in my dream? Frightened … I'm sure. But would I have had enough sense to believe and to act in faith? I can only speculate. However if I'm walking close to God and expecting to hear from Him, a messenger in a dream would surely have a positive effect on me.

Reflections

1. Nothing zaps the joy out of Christmas like betrayal. If you know someone who has suffered through betrayal, think of ways you can bring joy to his/her Christmas.

2. If you feel betrayed and have consequently lost your Christmas joy, ask God to show you ways to overcome your heartache.

3. How do you think you'd respond if He sent an answer via an angel?

Prayer

Heavenly Father, circumstances beyond my control threaten to zap my joy this Christmas season. Show me ways to overcome my concerns and bring You glory through them. In Jesus' name, amen.

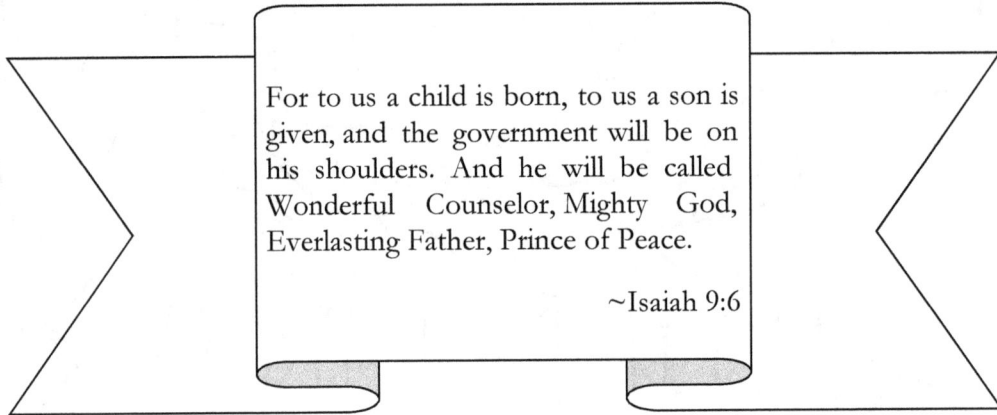

For to us a child is born, to us a son is given, and the government will be on his shoulders. And he will be called Wonderful Counselor, Mighty God, Everlasting Father, Prince of Peace.

~Isaiah 9:6

What's in a Name?

Names have meanings. Now there's a revelation for you. As if you didn't already know that, right? For most of us, when it comes to choosing names for babies, much consideration goes into it. God chose the name for His Son with great care. The name Jesus literally means, "God saves" or "YAHWEH is salvation."

When my husband and I were expecting our children, we named our daughters after people we admired, never considering the names' meanings. Nevertheless, the names we chose fit our daughters to a T. Not only that, my own name describes me pretty well too. I imagine many people have discovered the same thing. Coincidence? I doubt it. I believe God knew exactly who we'd each become, what our characteristics would be, and what we'd be interested in. Therefore, He prompted our parents subconsciously to give us names that would coincide with our biological makeup.

Regardless of your take on this subject, God prompted Joseph to name Mary's son Jesus. The name "Jesus" comes from a Greek translation of the Aramaic short form עוֹשׁ (Yeshu'a), which was the real name of Jesus and is also translated Joshua in the Old Testament. God sent His Son Jesus to save the world from sin and punishment. And that He did on the cross.

Yet, God also called His Son by other names such as the ones mentioned in the above verse. Each one tells of His majesty. Each one paints a different picture of the Son of God. Each one is unique to Jesus the Messiah.

Reflections

1. What do the names of Jesus in Isaiah 9:6 tell you about Him?

2. Read Revelation 19:12. Jesus has a name written on Him that no one knows but He Himself. God has a name for His Son not yet revealed … a name to which no one else will answer. It must be a marvelous name to describe the King of kings and Lord of lords, the Lamb of God, the Word of God, the Light of the World, the Savior. One name that completely identifies the Alpha and Omega. That must be quite a special name.

3. Do you know you are so special to God that He has a unique name for you too? It's written on a white stone and no one else in all of His kingdom will be known by your name (Revelation 2:17 NIV). Your name will describe you perfectly and be as unique as you are. What a wonderful God and Heavenly Father we serve.

Prayer

Loving Father, You have expressed Your affection for me in more ways than I can count or imagine. Yet, the greatest gift You have given me is acceptance into Your family. And to think You have sealed that promise by choosing a name uniquely mine. I am overwhelmed with joy. In Jesus' name, amen.

All this took place to fulfill what the Lord had said through the prophet: "The virgin will conceive and give birth to a son, and they will call him Immanuel" (which means "God with us").

~Isaiah 7:14 AMP

God with Us

My six-year-old granddaughter, Sydney, enjoys having sleepovers at Bee and Pap's house. When she was younger, she insisted I sleep with her. Now, she prefers sleeping in the living room on the floor … as long as I keep my bedroom door open. She needs to know Bee and Pap are close by, ready and willing to hold her should the need arise in the middle of the night.

Like Sydney, I derive comfort knowing someone cares enough to stay close and hold me when circumstances overwhelm me. However, I discovered no one can fulfill that role 100% of the time. No one that is, but Immanuel.

God with us. God is with me. Wow! What a thought.

When Jesus walked the dirt paths of Judea, people literally lived in the presence of God. They touched Him. More importantly, He touched them. He healed the sick among them, cast out demons , forgave their sins, calmed the storms at sea, and taught them about His Heavenly Father. He proved His deity through signs and wonders. The most significant, of course, was His power over death. Several times, He raised people from the dead, Lazarus being the most notable due to the length of time he lay dead in the tomb. But the greatest of all signs and wonders was His death on the cross where He suffered for our sins, which was climaxed by His resurrection from the dead three days later.

In doing so, Jesus Christ remains Immanuel—"God with Us." Because Jesus lives eternally, our object of worship extends beyond religion to relationship.

To me, Immanuel means I have access to my Wonderful Counselor when I'm confused. In times of despair, the Prince of Peace comforts me. I have a Father who disciplines me when I fall short of His will and holds me close when others fall short of my expectations. Jesus is all I need because of His never - ending, unconditional love for me. He sheds His light on my path so I don't lose my way and into my heart so that I know the areas on which He needs to work. He gives me His word that I may live by His assurance that I have a place of comfort and rest. I have a relationship with the King of kings and the Lord of lords. He calls me His friend, His beloved, His daughter. Furthermore, knowing God is with me always prompts me to conduct myself as a child of the King. While that means certain restrictions apply to my behavior, it also means my spirit soars in freedom from the bondage of sin and guilt.

Reflections

1. Immanuel— "God with Us." What comfort we can derive for that knowledge. How has Immanuel helped you through difficult situations?

2. How do you conduct yourself differently knowing God is with you always and everywhere?

3. Praise Him for His everlasting presence.

Prayer:

Heavenly Father, through Jesus—Immanuel, You have made Yourself available to the world … to me. You are my comfort, my peace, my joy. I celebrate Your advent and worship You for You are worthy, oh Lord, to receive honor and glory, and power. Amen.

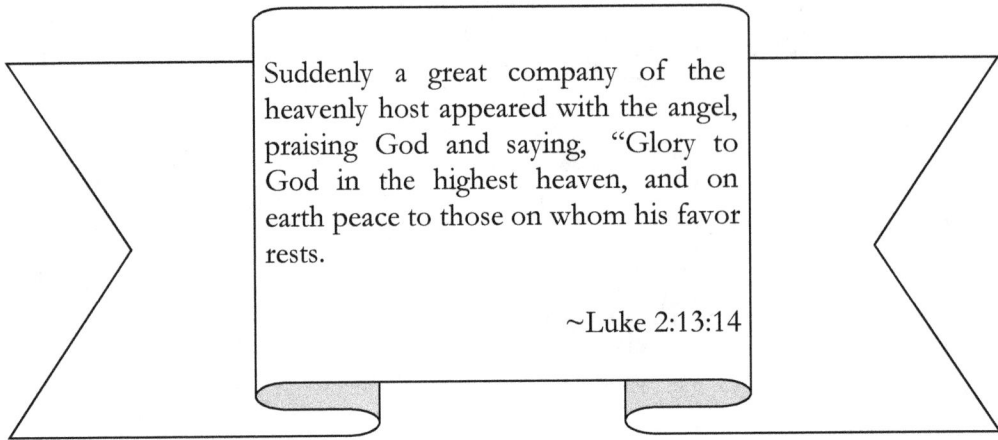

Suddenly a great company of the heavenly host appeared with the angel, praising God and saying, "Glory to God in the highest heaven, and on earth peace to those on whom his favor rests.

~Luke 2:13:14

Angels We Have Seen

Typically, shepherds brought their flocks together at night into a rocky area that was enclosed on three sides so the sheep wouldn't wonder off. Then the shepherds drew straws for the watch. They guarded the sheep like soldiers on the city gate. They each had, most likely, come face-to-face with more than one beast. Therefore, the shepherds on duty would have stayed wide-eyed and alert. They anticipated tackling a 700-pound bear or chasing off a 420-pound lion. But an angel? The sighting couldn't have been a hallucination. No way! No two people see the exact same vision at the exact same moment even if they're under the influence of drugs that induce hallucinations. Not to mention the message … . Everyone heard the message. Add to the excitement and drama a multitude of angels too numerous to count singing a chorus of praise to Almighty God and you've got the formula for an inexplicable event. That's what the shepherds experienced the night Jesus was born.

At the risk of being presumptuous, I doubt that a college football stadium (average capacity 100,000) filled with the world's best vocalists singing praises would sound much better than croaking frogs compared to the sound the shepherds heard. Furthermore, the Northern Lights or the most gorgeous sunrise would be little more than a field of fireflies in comparison to what the shepherds saw.

I can't begin to imagine the mixed emotions the shepherds must have felt. Fear … most assuredly. Excitement mingled with wonder. Curiosity coupled with paralyzing tremors.

Perhaps I would've thought I was dreaming until I saw the fear in the other shepherds' faces. Then I probably would've trembled in awesome wonder at the realization that angels from the Most High were serenading us. Someone else would've had to suggest we go to Bethlehem to see the miracle. I would've been speechless for quite some time.

Reflections

1. Shepherds in Biblical times understood the dangers threatening their flocks and kept close watch during the night. How do you watch over those whom you hold most dear?

2. As the event unfolds, the shepherds heeded the angel's advice, went to Bethlehem in search of the Christ-child, and told everyone about the miracle they witnessed. To whom can you tell about Jesus?

3. God delights in revealing His love for us, even though He uses methods somewhat less extravagant as serenading angels. Sometimes, He uses the commonplace things —like a special sale on art supplies—to affirm His affections for us. When I realized He guided me to that sale, it made my heart sing. What has God done for you recently that made your heart sing?

Prayer

Heavenly Father, Your display of love even in the mundane things makes my heart sing. Show me ways to share Your love with those around me this Christmas. In Jesus' name, amen.

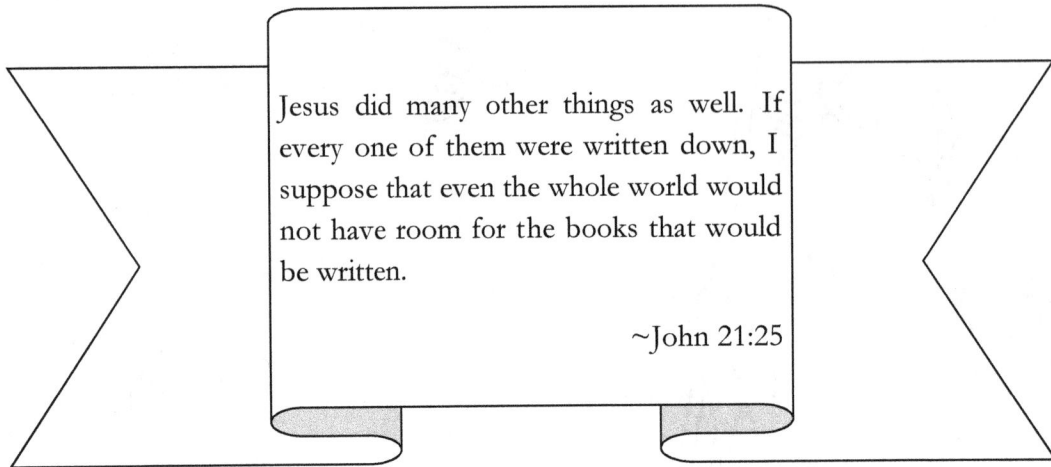

Jesus did many other things as well. If every one of them were written down, I suppose that even the whole world would not have room for the books that would be written.

~John 21:25

The Most Amazing Thing about Jesus

In the past two thousand years, there have been scores of books written about Jesus Christ. But none of them have recorded anything new that Jesus had done while He walked the dusty paths of Judea. It's been enough for humanity to consider what has already been recorded about Him. Still, can you imagine the many miracles and teachings He had done in just three years that compelled the Apostle John, an eyewitness, to write the world couldn't hold the books if everything Jesus did had been written down?

Amazing? Indeed, but it's not the most amazing thing about Jesus.

Jesus was God incarnate … God in the flesh. That's like you or me becoming an amoeba to save a world of microscopic, single-cell creatures who neither know nor care anything about us. Imagine giving up all the freedom and vast array of abilities you have to become a microscopic, single-cell creature. Imagine those creatures wanting to make you their political leader, then turning against you when you refuse the office. Imagine them spitting on you, beating you, and torturing you to death. Imagine coming back to life in their realm to show them your authority and having them reject you still. Imagine doing all that knowing beforehand what would take place. That's what Jesus did when He came to earth as a man.

Incomprehensible? Yes, but it's not the most amazing thing about Jesus.

From the beginning, Jesus was with God and in fact, was God. By Him and for Him all things were created. Jesus is the Light of the world. In Him there is no darkness. In Him is life from which all living things generate their existence.

Unimaginable? Absolutely, yet it's not the most amazing thing about Jesus.

Even if I'd been the only person in the universe throughout all history who believed and accepted God's gift of salvation, Jesus would have come to earth to take on the sins of the entire human race. Although I'm at times ungrateful … although I'm most unworthy … although I was hopeless … although I was dead in my sin (Ephesians 2:1) … although I've done nothing to deserve it nor can I do anything to repay Him, Jesus loves me and died for me.

That's the most amazing thing about Jesus.

Reflections

1. The gospels of Matthew and Luke record some pretty amazing events surrounding Jesus ' birth. Which one is your favorite?

2. What's the most amazing event that happened to you during the advent season?

3. Although you may have experienced some truly amazing things in your life, nothing compares to the most amazing thing about Jesus. Does He love you that much? Oh yes, He does!

Prayer:

Heavenly Father, it's difficult for me to wrap my mind around Your everlasting, enduring, unconditional, amazing love for me. But it makes my heart sing with gratitude. In Jesus' name, amen.

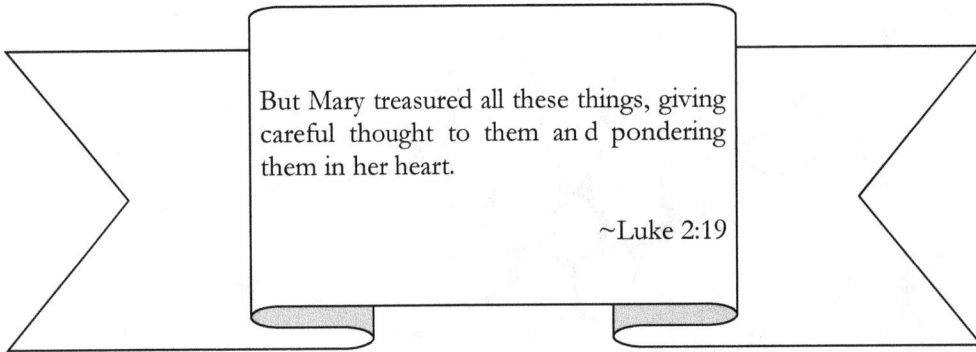

But Mary treasured all these things, giving careful thought to them an d pondering them in her heart.

~Luke 2:19

Much More to Christmas

We all enjoy presents with ribbons and tags,
Giving and getting gifts, boxes, and bags;
So, what shall I give? Do I dare ask for more?
And what do I spend on each gift at the store?
I've shopped, and I ache from my head to my feet,
I'm tired of smiling at folks whom I meet;
Happy I'll be when the garland's all hung,
I wish it was o'er, and the last song was sung.
Then, with my bustling, I've thought, Is it true?
Could Christmas mean much more to me and to you?

Door bells ringing
Laughing and singing
Friends and caring
Memory sharing
Talking, joking
Tender rib poking
Susan and Joe
Beneath mistletoe
Good will greetings
Parties, church meetings.

But there is much, much more; I give you my word;
There's much more to Christmas, or haven't you heard?
An angel met Mary, the virgin and blessed
Then stood before Joseph to cheer and impress,
"Take Mary to wife and the child as your own;
He one day will rule from his heavenly throne."
On a hill, humble shepherds watched sheep late that night,
And heard angels chorus God's promise with delight;
The glory of God turned the dark into day
While Jesus the Babe fell asleep on the hay;
The Savior became a compassionate man
With marvelous healing in both of his hands.

Mercy and grace
Glorified His face
People believed
Miracles received
Burdens lifted
Then tempers shifted
A crown of thorns
Soldiers' hateful scorns
Hung on a cross
Suffering and loss

His sacrifice made, he was laid in a tomb;
The whole Earth did mourn over three days of gloom.
But then God, His Father, said, "Come out, my Son!
Rejoice and be glad for the victory's won!"
The first Christmas Day the best gift had been giv'n,
And Jesus still lives, so my sins are forgiven.
As long as I live, I will spend all my days
Rejoicing and singing and shouting His praise;
I've seen it, I've felt it, I know it is true,
Yes, Christmas means much more to me and to you.

Reflections

1. The Christmas frenzy can even weary children. How can you slow the pace enough to refresh their spirits and reflect on what Christmas means?

2. It's Sunday. Time to rest. Instead of planning next week's events, use the time to ponder, as Mary did, the events that surrounded Jesus' birth.

3. Enjoy your fellowship with God … relax … pray … nap.

Prayer

Heaven Father, thank you for this moment to ponder You love, Your birth, Your serenity. In Jesus' name, amen.

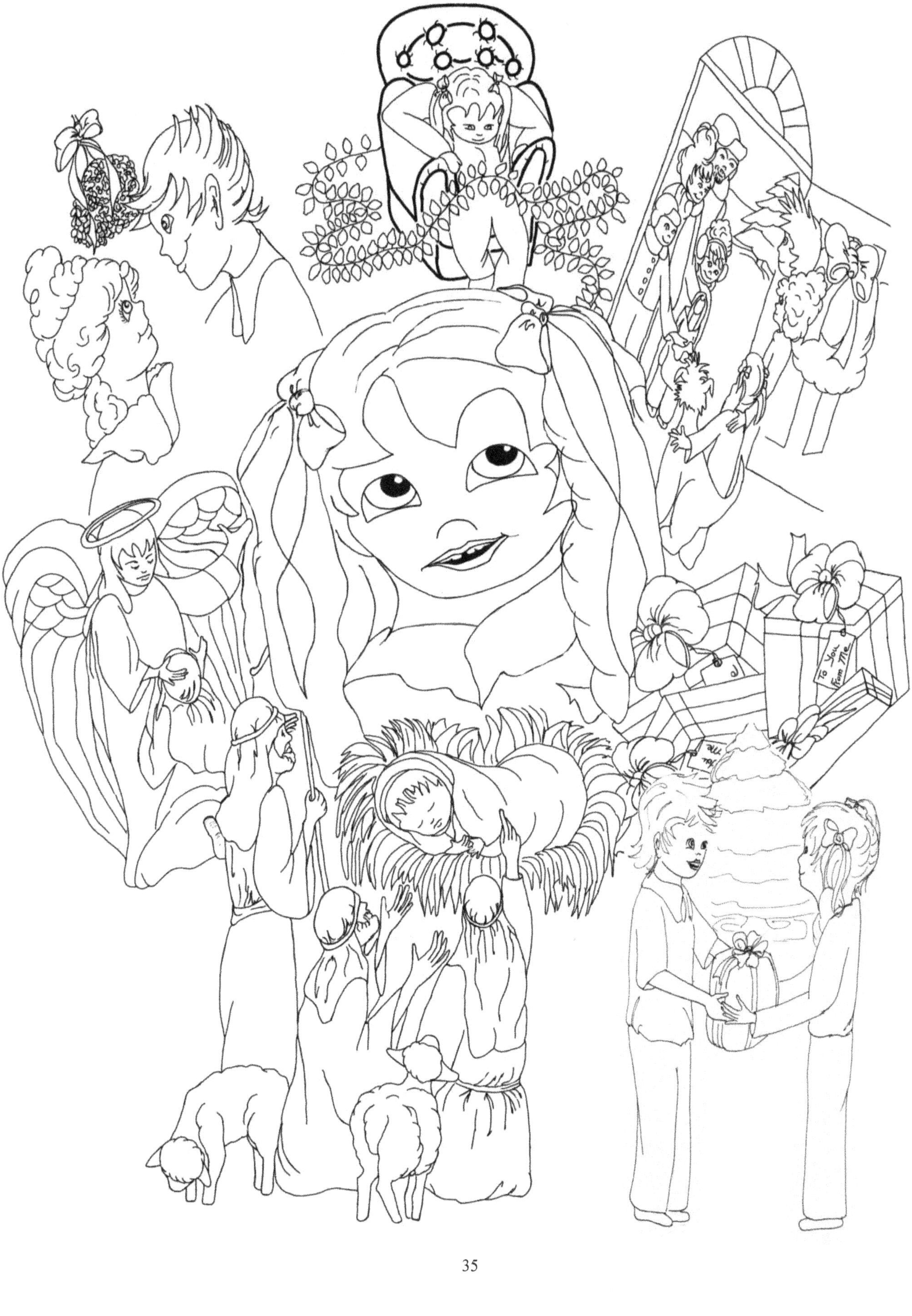
To You From Me

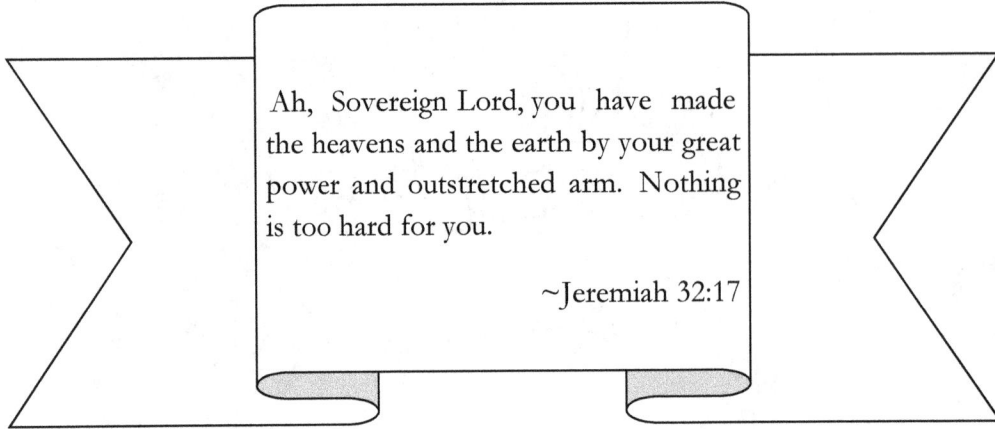

Ah, Sovereign Lord, you have made the heavens and the earth by your great power and outstretched arm. Nothing is too hard for you.

~Jeremiah 32:17

Christmas Lists

Impossible challenges float from the sky like snowflakes at Christmastime. I plan. I design. I procrastinate. I go to lunch with friends. I shop with my mother. I fall behind schedule. Now with the big day closing in, I have homemade gifts to complete, cookies to bake, and an art video to finish. Oh, and did I mention gifts to wrap … if I get them finished.

These projects only rank on the impossibility list because of my own negligence. But Christmas sheds light on areas of life over which we have no control. We scurry through the season trying to forget, or at least minimize our concerns for a brief time. Nevertheless, health issues deplete our energy. Broken relationships zap our strength. Lack of income squelches our giving spirits. This list seems endless and hopeless. The cumbersome woes of this world flicker like flames on a candle. Although it is impossible for us to extinguish them, God is able to snuff them out and restore the joy of the season with just a breath.

He proves His ability to perform the unimaginable with His own list of impossibilities that emerges at Christmastime … an angel speaking to a young maiden, an angel in a dream, a trusting husband, a babe born of a virgin, a choir of angels on a hillside, shepherds seeking, a star guiding, Magi kneeling. All arranged by God's hand because God delights in doing the impossible.

Reflections

1. Christmas is a time for making lists. Grocery lists grow longer as we plan the menu for family gatherings and our baking needs. Lists of gifts for special people seem endless. And then there's the matter of what to include on our personal "want list." But have you considered your list of impossibilities this Christmas? Have you given them to the God who delights in doing the impossible?

2. In today's economy, our children's lists, including electronic toys and designer clothes, stamp our shopping lists with a big, bold IMPOSSIBLE. But they don't have to dampen our giving spirits. Try explaining to your children about the expense and the economy. Even small children learn to understand and accept they can't have everything they ask for when we take time to explain why.

3. God does not give us everything we ask for either. Some things on our impossibility lists are meant for our good. And even though God is able to do what is impossible for us, He knows what is best for us, what will strengthen us, and what will draw us closer to Him. When we give our impossibility list to the God who delights in doing the impossible, He gives us His best, not our desires.

Prayer

Heavenly Father, I want to celebrate the birth of Your Son with enthusiasm and joy. But my list of impossibilities has stifled my zest for the season. I relinquish my list into Your hands, trusting You to do what You do best—the impossible. In Jesus' name, amen.

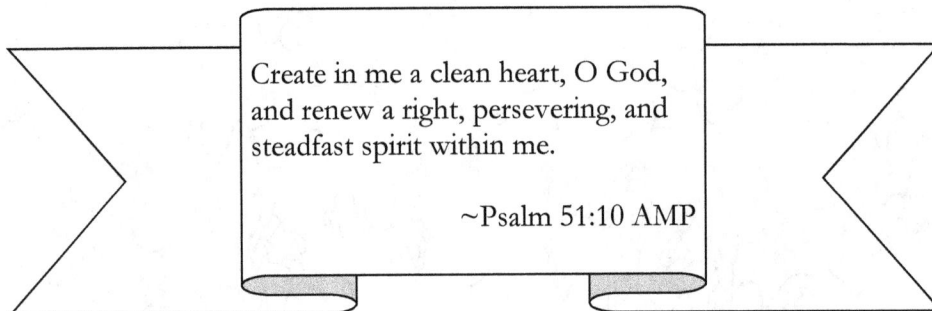

Create in me a clean heart, O God, and renew a right, persevering, and steadfast spirit within me.

~Psalm 51:10 AMP

A New Creation in Christ Jesus

Creating snow people bears a striking resemblance to God at work in us. Scripture says He created us in our mothers' wombs (Psalm 139:13), but He didn't stop there. He invites us to come to Him through faith in Jesus. When we do, a new creation begins (2 Corinthians 5:17).

When I was growing up, Christmastime meant snow and lots of it. My brother and I built snow forts for snowball battles and snowmen. In fact, we made entire snow families in our backyard. Starting with a hand-sized snowball, we rolled it around the yard until it grew into a huge mound for the base. Then we made the middle snowball about two-thirds the size of the first. Finally we made the head, topped it with a knit hat, coal eyes and mouth, and yes, a carrot nose. Our snowmen looked like every other snowman in our neighborhood.

But as we grew older, we got more creative. Our snow people had arms shaped from snow, not mere twigs. Their heads grew ears, obvious cheeks, and yes, lips. Of course, they had to have hair, so we sculpted that in also. We worked hard to make them resemble us, their creators.

God created humans in His own image according to Genesis chapter two. But after the fall of man, God's image melted within our souls like a snowman on a warm day. Nevertheless, He didn't stop loving us. Instead, He devised a plan that involved sending His only Son to die for our sins. When we accept the gift of salvation, God begins working on a new creation in us. Through circumstances, both good and bad, He replaces negative attitudes, inappropriate desires, and selfish motives with positive attributes, Godly desires, and selfless giving. His sole desire is to restore His image within us.

Reflections

1. God's still working on me. I can tell because I appreciate people more than I used to, even when they don't live up to my expectations. How have you sensed God's creative hand on your life as He develops a Christlike image in you?

2. While God is busy creating a Christlike image in you, think of some creative ways you can share the changes He has made in your life.

3. As my husband matures in Christ, he doesn't get as flustered with things that go on at work. At least, he's learning to keep his negative comments to himself instead of unleashing his frustrations on the offender. If you've noticed any positive changes in a fellow believer, send them a card complimenting them on their progress, especially if the person is a new Christian. Encouragement is one of the best gifts we can give.

Prayer

Heavenly Father, I know You're working on me, although it's difficult at times to see the changes You've made. Help me not only to see my own progress, but to see the progress of others so that I may encourage them. In Jesus' name, amen.

The people walking in darkness have seen a great light; on those living in the land of deep darkness a light has dawned.

~Isaiah 9:2

Christmas Lights

Children from three to ninety-three gaze at the awesome displays of festive Christmas lights that illuminate practically every street. What is it about Christmas lights that enchant us so? Could it be they commemorate the sighting of the angels by the shepherds on the hillside the night Jesus was born? Or the star that led the wise men from the Far East to the King of kings? I suppose they represent different ideas to different people. Nevertheless, Christmas lights add gaiety to the season and bring pleasure to many people who otherwise find little enjoyment in Yuletide.

Travel with me down such a street. Ooh and ah at the sights. Some yards glitter with sleighs, deer, and snowmen all made of wires and white lights. Others display Santas, giant gifts, and Christmas trees all shimmering with a rainbow of lights. Still others exhibit manger scenes—life-size Marys, Josephs, donkeys shepherds, wise men, and sheep bow their heads toward the infants nestled in the mangers. They too glisten with lights, some from within, some from without. At the intersection, we turn the corner with anticipation, but our hearts sink. The street is dark for as far as we can see. We motor on hoping to find more displays. To our dismay, there are none, not even an ordinary streetlight. We head home.

The dark road serves as a cruel reminder that not much life exists in the absence of light. Is it any wonder that darkness is synonymous with the lack of moral and spiritual values?

Although darkness holds great power, even the tiny glow of a firefly extinguishes it momentarily by God's design. Bring on greater light and darkness must flee.

Similarly, spiritual light obliterates the iniquity within the human soul. Religious "lights" illuminate the need for moral standards. They reflect guidelines of conduct to secure a safe environment in which to live. But like Christmas lights, these moral lights only simulate the real light God has provided for humanity. That Light is Jesus Christ. In Him, no darkness nor shadows exist. He alone completely extingu ishes darkness. Those who walk in His light often live more courageously, full of hope and zeal for life.

Through Jesus Christ, we too become the light of the world to illuminate the path for others so they, too, can find their way to Him.

Reflections

1. Christmas lights add a lot of sparkle to the long, dark December nights, reminding us of the spiritual light that came into the world in the person of Jesus Christ. With whom can you share the Light?

2. The Bible says the Light came into the world, but the world, although created by Him, did not recognize Him (John 1:10). Later, Jesus said, "Light has come into the world, but people loved darkness instead of light because their deeds were evil" (John 3:19). Don't criticize. Don't judge. Show respect. Show love. And pray to become an effective Light bearer.

3. Jesus also said believers are the light of the world (Matthew 5:14). Similar to hanging Christmas lights, God has purposely placed each of us in our communities to add sparkle to this dark world. How can you let your light shine for Jesus this Christmas?

Prayer

Heavenly Father, thank You for decorating my heart with the Light of Jesus. Show me ways to let my light reflect the greater Light so others would recognize Jesus. In His name, I pray. Amen.

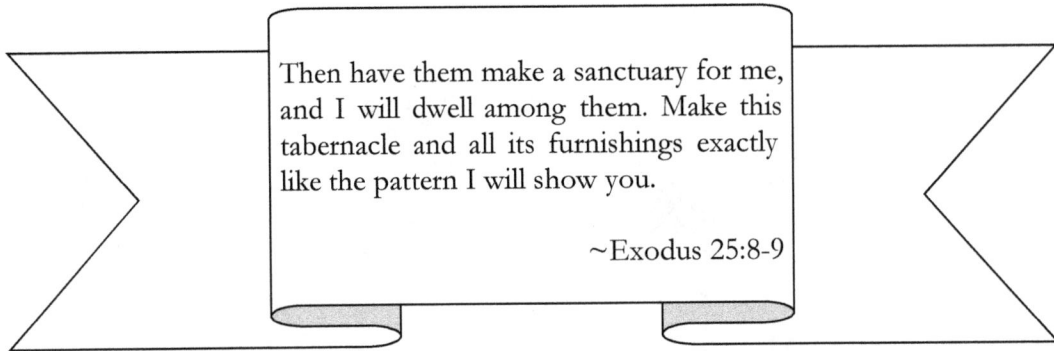

Then have them make a sanctuary for me, and I will dwell among them. Make this tabernacle and all its furnishings exactly like the pattern I will show you.

~Exodus 25:8-9

Let's Decorate

"Let's plan a birthday party for Eric. He'll be four in a few weeks, and his parents are both unemployed." My neighbor Sandra practically burst into my living room that day. Her eyes twinkled with anticipation. "We have to think of the coolest theme ever."

"Okay." I agreed. "How about Bob the Builder? My grandsons loved that character when they were that age."

"That might be a little harsh. Eric's father was a construction worker, you know. He got a permanent pink slip two weeks ago."

"Sorry. I didn't know his situation was permanent." I tapped the table as I often do when thinking. "Clowns. Everyone loves clowns. And I just happened to know…"

"Not everyone." Sandra shook her head. "Eric's one of those little guys who's deathly afraid of the Bozos and Ronald McDonalds of the world."

"What about Superman, Spiderman, or the Hulk." I struck my best Incredible Hulk pose. Sandra grinned, but shook her head to that suggestion too.

"He calls them all weird. And don't you dare suggest Batman. The boy's just not into superheroes."

"Wow! He is a tough one."

"Yeah. But we have to make it special for him. His family has been through so much lately. Did you know their dog got hit on the road the other day?"

It was my turn to shake my head.

"It didn't kill her outright; but with both parents out of work, their only option was to put her down.

"Poor little Eric." I poured us each a cup of coffee and returned to the table. "What about an amusement park theme?"

"Oh that's perfect. He went to Knoebel's Grove Amusement Park this summer and couldn't stop talking about it. I knew you'd come up with a great idea." Sandra sipped her coffee. "Let the planning begin."

*****

This little scenario demonstrates most of our desires to plan a birthday party for the pleasure of the honored guest. But do we take as much consideration when decorating for Christmas. God expects us to honor and glorify His Son, especially when we say we belong to Jesus and desire to celebrate His advent.

Reflections

1. Inventory your decorations. What do they mean to you? How do they honor Jesus? Would He be delighted in the choices you've made in preparation of His birthday celebration?

2. If some ornaments hold a special memory, share it with your family and guests. As you trim your tree, reflect on Christmases past. While you set up your nativity, think about the role each person represented played on that first Christmas Eve.

3. Think of other ways you can keep Jesus in the center of the celebration this year.

Prayer

Heavenly Father, show me ways to bring honor and glory to Jesus as I celebrate His first advent and look forward to His second coming. In His precious name, I pray. Amen.

But when the set time had fully come, God sent his Son, born of a woman, born under the law, to redeem those under the law, that we might receive adoption to sonship.

~Galatians 4:4-5

The Reason for the Season

Jesus is the Reason for the Season signs and stickers pop up everywhere this time of year. They serve as nice reminders of the meaning of Christmas. But they have gotten it all wrong. According to scripture, PEOPLE ARE THE REASON FOR THE SEASON … you and I.

We are the lost sheep Jesus came to seek and to save. He humbled Himself for us and entered a small world, in comparison to His kingdom, which was created by His own hands. He lived to show us how to serve others, respond to our enemies, and glorify the Father. He died to cleanse us from the filth of our sins in preparation for adoption into His family. He rose again to affirm our inheritance.

The day we accept Jesus' offer for salvation, God accepts us as His sons and daughters. That makes us royalty—princes and princesses.

As a child, I loved to pretend I was a princess. I never really believed I would become one. I simply found pretending to belong to a special family everyone admired a lot of fun. It wasn't until I became an adult that I understood the truth of my play acting. Psalm 139 says I am "fearfully and wonderfully made." Romans 8:15-17 reminds me that I have been adopted and can now call God—Abba Father. Not only that, I am an heir of God and co-heir with Jesus as the above verse also proclaims.

Unfortunately, I don't always act like a princess. Sometimes I drift away and play in the "dirt" like a little waif. Sometimes I think I know better than my Father. I try to tell Him how to handle situations I know little or nothing about. Sometimes I tremble in fear for lack of trust in His sovereignty. Sometimes I get spunky and refuse to do His bidding. Sometimes in full awareness of His will, I run ahead to accomplish the task before it is time, thereby risking complications in God's plan or neglecting what should be done now.

Nevertheless my Father remains faithful, just, and patient. If I need disciplined, He does so in love. He always forgives me, cleans my "soiled garment," and sets me on a higher rock. He promised to never leave me, lose me, or reject me.

I'm glad my adoption certificate is in His hands, signed in Jesus' blood, and sealed in the Holy Spirit.

Reflections

1. How does thinking you are the "reason for the season" make you feel?

2. Although the season is all about us, we don't have the right to focus on ourselves at Christmas or during any other season. How can you place more of your focus on Jesus and less on the world?

3. Christmas often means parties. And parties often bring out the waifs in us rather than the prince or princess. How can you modify your behavior to portray the prince or princess you really are in Christ?

Prayer

Heavenly Father, help me to focus on the real reason for the season by treating others like royalty rather than worrying so much about my lengthy to-do list. In Jesus' name, amen.

"Vanity of vanities," says the Preacher. "Vanity of vanities! All [that is done without God's guidance] is vanity [futile, meaningless—a wisp of smoke, a vapor that vanishes, merely chasing the wind]."

Ecclesiastes 1:2

Con Sumer's Black Friday Blitz (Part 1)

At midnight, Con Sumer entered the department store and wove his way through the crowd, whistling *Here Comes Santa Claus*. He stopped abruptly in front of the display ... the empty display.

What? The store wasn't supposed to open until midnight. Con checked his watch—12:03 a.m. *How can the shelves be empty already?*

"Clerk!" Con tapped a nearby sales-rep on the shoulder and pointed at the empty display. "Where's the super-duper-special-priced robot kit?"

"That's the number one item this year. So they got scarfed up the minute the store opened."

"But ..." Con pointed to his watch.

"Guess you'll have to get here earlier next year."

"Earlier? I got here precisely at midnight ... the time stated on the ad."

"Well everyone knows the doors open fifteen minutes before the ad time."

The rep's voice trailed off as Con scurried around the end of the counter. Apparently, neither store managers nor shopaholics regarded rules, like opening the doors at the time advertised, as being a necessary part of the shopping frenzy.

Isn't there a code of ethics among bargain hunters? Even thieves have a code of ethics.

Con pushed up his sleeves, squared his shoulders, and marched deeper into the store battlefront ready to take on the world of crazed shopaholics. He deserved those price-cuts as much as anyone. His kids and wife deserved an extravagant Christmas.

With a white-knuckled grip, Con pushed his cart through the crowd to the game department. Three people rammed their carts into his shins. Carelessness or an attempt to move him, he couldn't tell. But if they wanted to play demolition derby with shopping carts, he was game. He grabbed an X-WII-Tendo something or other for his twelve-year-old son Rob. Then he rushed to the toy aisle, crashing into the cart of a woman who took up more than her share of the space in front of the doll display. Then he spied it ... the doll, or at least a reasonable facsimile, on his six-year-old daughter Edie's list ... the last one on the shelf. He and the woman grabbed the box at the same time. The woman tugged. Con grunted in disgust, yanked it out of her hand, and plopped it in his cart. The woman reached for it.

"Don't even think about." Con scowled and marched to the register. On the way, he picked up a watch for the missus, a football for Rob, and a frying pan he had no clue what to do with.

A ribbon of florescent pink streaked the horizon as Con pulled into his driveway with a trunk full of purchases, a credit card full of charges, and shins full of bruises. But other than the do-it-yourself robot thing, he managed to get every single item on his list, plus some things he never intended to buy. What a Christmas this promised to be.

(Read the conclusion of Con Sumer's Black Friday Blitz in tomorrow's devotion.)

Reflections

1. Christmas shopping brought out the beast in Con, ending in a "chasing of the wind" as King Solomon would say. How could Con have tamed the beast othe r than not shopping on Black Friday?

2. My first experience with Black Friday shopping at midnight proved enjoyable. But things other than shopping unleash my Christmas beast. What brings out your Christmas beast?

3. Reread the above verse from Ecclesiastes. What does the Preacher suggest we do to avoid the "chasing of the wind?"

Prayer

Heavenly Father, help me to put things into perspective and seek Your guidance in all things so that I don't "chase after the wind" this Christmas. In Jesus' name, amen.

When anxiety was great within me, your consolation brought me joy.

~Psalm 94:19

Con Sumer's Black Friday Blitz (part 2)

Christmas morning, floorboards creaked as Rob and Edie sneaked into the living room peeked at the gifts beneath the tree, and crept back upstairs. Then a ray of light broad ened as the kids opened their parents' bedroom door.

"Mommy! Daddy!" Edie squealed. "Wake up. It's Christmas."

Martha and Con moaned, pretending not to be interested, and rolled over.

"Come on." Rob shook the bed. "Get up."

Martha shrugged on her housecoat. "Okay. Let's get this show on the road."

Con followed his family to the tree and, taking his usual seat, picked up a package. "To Rob, From Santa."

Rob smirked. "Dad, seriously. Santa?" He grabbed the present and ripped it open. "I have this game."

Martha sighed and shook her head "You can exchange it tomorrow, dear."

"Okay," Rob said. "Thanks, Dad."

Con nodded. With his joy a little deflated, he remembered the carts-to-the-shins he'd endured to get that game. He forced a smile and picked up another present. "To Edie, From Santa."

Edie clapped her hands. "I love Santa," she said as she grabbed the gift and tore it open. Her grin shriveled into a grimace. "This isn't a chatty Suzy. It's … it's a fake." Edie tossed the doll on the floor and whimpered.

Guilt prickled Con's heart as the vision of the battle for that doll replayed in his mind. "I'm sorry, honey. It was the only doll left on the display rack. We can take it back tomorrow and you can choose one."

"Really? I can pick it out?"

"Yes."

The kids seemed genuinely appreciative of the rest of their gifts. And Martha adored her watch. But Con dreaded the thought of facing another crazed-shopper day in lines of exchanges and refunds tomorrow. He picked up the doll and video game, placed them in a shopping bag, and set them on top of the piano. Laughter from the other room turned Con's head in that direction.

"Con, aren't you gonna join us?" Martha called. "We're playing Snap the Dragon."

"My favorite game." Con rushed to the family room and sat on the floor beside Edie.

She kissed his cheek. "I love you, Daddy. And I love playing Snap the Dragon 'cause I always win."

Con grinned. Why had he thought joining the crazed shopaholics Black Friday would make their Christmas special? This was what he'd been shopping for … this happiness. Funny, it had been here all along in their family time, in their hugs and kisses, in their laughter, and yeah, even in the disappointments. This was true Christmas joy.

Reflections

1. Like poor Con Sumer, many of us feel somewhat empty at the end of the season. Spending quality time with family and friends can fill that void. Consider going technology-free all Christmas Day to connect with those you love.

2. Dealing with the "that's-not-what-I-wanted" syndrome can put a damper on the festivities. How can you handle the disappointment without letting it ruin your day?

3. Simple things, like laughter, hugs, and time spent together, become valued memories long after the toys, electronics, and designer clothes disappear. Make a list of things that made you laugh this year, tuck it in your Bible, and read it periodically throughout the year.

Prayer

Heavenly Father, thank You for laughter, hugs, and family In Jesus' name, amen.

On coming to the house, they [the Magi] saw the child with his mother Mary, and they bowed down and worshiped him. Then they opened their treasures and presented him with gifts of gold, frankincense and myrrh.

~Matthew 2:11

Reverence the King of Kings

Humility is not an American attribute. Of course many Americans are humble, but for the most part, we're known for arrogance and rudeness around the world. Many show little respect for authority, let alone understand the importance of paying homage to a king. Our culture teaches that all men and women are created equal. Therefore, our high officials receive the same greeting as the local plumber or salesperson. We know nothing of bowing before anyone who holds an office.

While Americans can be overbearingly prideful and disrespectful, we don't hold a monopoly on the careless attitude toward authority. People around the globe are arrogant toward God. Even Christians have become so "friendly" with our Savior that we've lost our fear and respect for Him. In essence, when we lose our reverence of God, we become lax and sloppy in our worship. We shrug off His laws. We begin to do what seems right in our own eyes. Sound familiar? Look up Judges 21:25. In those days, everyone did as they saw fit with no regard to God or His laws. They had no king and lived in total chaos.

Chaos abounds in the world today. We need to develop fear and respect for the government officials who help maintain law and order on earth. While we're at it, we need to reverence the King of kings like the Magi did as recorded in Matthew's gospel.

Being astrologers, the Magi recognized a new, significant star. Convinced that it denoted the birth of a king, they followed it to Jerusalem and eventually to Bethlehem. These wise men realized the importance of paying homage to the king—any king. They had no way of knowing that the child before whom they knelt was the King of kings. Nevertheless, they revered Him. They brought expensive gifts as tokens of their admiration, respect, and fear.

We would do well to imitate the Magi's attitudes and actions. Paul wrote to the Philippians, "that at the name of Jesus every knee should bow, in heaven and on earth and under the earth, and every tongue acknowledge that Jesus Christ is Lord, to the glory of God the Father" (2:10-11). We have a choice—humble ourselves now and pay homage to the King of kings out of obedience, love, respect, and reverent fear. Or one day, we'll be humiliated before His throne and drop to our knees in shame with dreadful fear and trembling.

Reflections

1. One of the ways we show respect to the King of kings in our day and culture is by showing respect to those in authority over us. This includes police officers. Wouldn't it be nice if we'd flood their mailboxes with Christmas cards stating our appreciation for their services?

2. Our bosses reign over us, some with an iron-clad fist. Nonetheless, God placed them in charge. A gift card to a local restaurant might add a little Christmas cheer to their lives. Who knows it might even mellow them out a bit.

3. How about the mayor of your town? Have you thought to send him/her a greeting with a note of appreciation? Until now, I haven't. It might brighten their day.

Prayer

Heavenly Father, I don't often think to express gratitude to those who serve as authoritative figures in my life. Thank You for placing them in office. Give them wisdom to carry out their roles and grant them safety. In Jesus' name, amen.

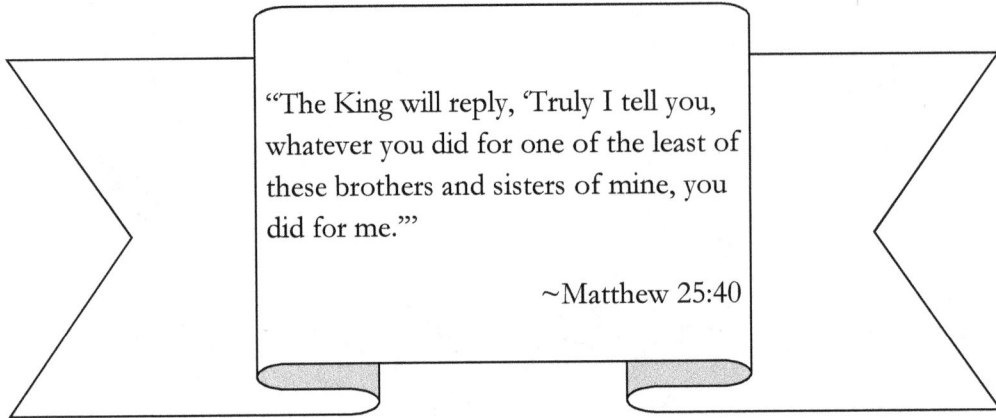

"The King will reply, 'Truly I tell you, whatever you did for one of the least of these brothers and sisters of mine, you did for me.'"

~Matthew 25:40

A Personal Touch

Christmas, the time of year when the spirit of giving prevails, prompts us to spend money as though we have no bills to pay the entire month of December or, in some cases, the entire next year.

Some charities take advantage of this giving frenzy, overstuffing our mailboxes and tying up our telephone lines. With the assurance that a grant will double our money, we make pledges to send relief to the needy across the world.

We make special trips to nursing homes and hospitals, send cards to shut-ins, and pack shoe boxes full of nonperishables for children in third-world countries. It's a good thing to give in Christ's name ... the one thing He has asked of us. The one thing we can truly give back to Him.

But what about the needy in our own communities? With all the unemployment and the funds running out, many people right here in Hometown, USA, need care packages. The elderly person across the street whose spouse has passed into eternity would probably appreciate a visit and a hug. The couple who lost their child to cancer might enjoy a night out to take their minds off their loss if only for an hour. Yes, we could buy them a gift certificate at a nice restaurant. However, wouldn't it be better to invite them to our homes for a meal and to play games?

Jesus said what we do to the least, the forgotten in our communities, we have done that very thing to Him.

Reflections

1. Most of us cherish the time spent with relatives and close friends. But what about that elderly person across the street who never seems to hav e company at Christmastime or any other time throughout the year? Could you extend the invitation to your family gathering to him/her?

2. Jesus told a parable about a king who prepared a great feast and invited all his relatives. They all declined the invitation. So the king sent word to his neighbors--the poor, the despicable, the outcasts. Jesus said, "Such is the kingdom of heaven." What can you do for the least popular people in your community this Christmas?

3. Last Christmas while eating in a small local restaurant, I noticed an elderly man in a tattered coat, sitting alone. He looked sad as he nibbled on his meager breakfast. When I paid for my husband's and my meals, I told the waitress to keep enough for the man's meal too. Teary-eyed, the man patted my husband's shoulder as he exited the restaurant. Paying for that man's meal was one of the best blessings I've ever received. Funny how that works. Blessings always come back at you like boomerangs. Look for someone to bless today.

Prayer

Heavenly Father, Christmas blessings are so much fuller when we give them from our hearts. Show me those who need a blessing today. In Jesus' name, amen.

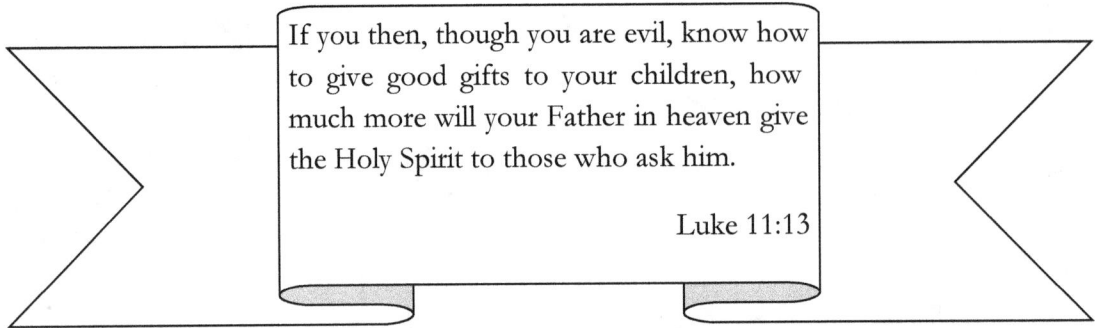

If you then, though you are evil, know how to give good gifts to your children, how much more will your Father in heaven give the Holy Spirit to those who ask him.

Luke 11:13

What Did You Get for Christmas?

What did you get for Christmas? The question buzzes everywhere you go for a week or so after the big day.

Funny how most of those "wonderful" gifts have been long forgotten. But the ones that I disliked receiving stick in my head, namely *the unmentionables*—socks and underwear. My childhood wish list never included the necessities. And I didn't like getting them one bit.

Nevertheless, our attitudes change with time. This year when my husband asked me what I wanted for Christmas, the only thing I could think of was … "I need socks." What? My socks were pretty worn out, and my feet get cold easily. There are only so many times you can darn them. My husband obliged much to my delight. I giggled as I remembered my dismay in opening socks on Christmas Days past.

As a child, I tagged along with my family to relatives' homes to see what was left under everyone's trees. We sat on their couches as one-by-one our cousins displayed their new toys, clothes, jewelry, or whatever they received. We spent a short time at each house to play. Then, that household would pack into their car and follow us to the next relative's home. By the time we returned to our house, we had a caravan of relatives following us. Into our living room the parade marched and sat around our Christmas tree as we showcased our new belongings.

Of course, our relatives never saw *the unmentionables.*

My parents gave us grand Christmases with what looked like a sleigh-full of gifts under the tree. Most of which were necessities such as socks, underwear, mittens, hats, and scarves. Soap, deodorant, and perfume filled stockings. Yes, the majority of our gifts fell on the list of necessities rather than on our wish lists. But my parents knew our needs and did their best to supply them.

Reflections

1. Have you noticed most of your best Christmas memories center around the emotion of the day and not the gifts received?

2. Add to those memories by asking each person at your family gathering to share happy moments from Christmases past.

3. We show our families our desire to supply their needs by presenting them with gifts. Likewise, the wondrous gift of God's love exemplifies His understanding of the human condition and His desire to meet our needs. He gave His best for those who were not yet called His sons and daughters. And God wraps us, the receivers, in His Holy Spirit as a gift back to Himself.

Prayer

Heavenly Father, thank You for your gift of salvation. Remind me to share it with others throughout the year. In Jesus' name, amen.

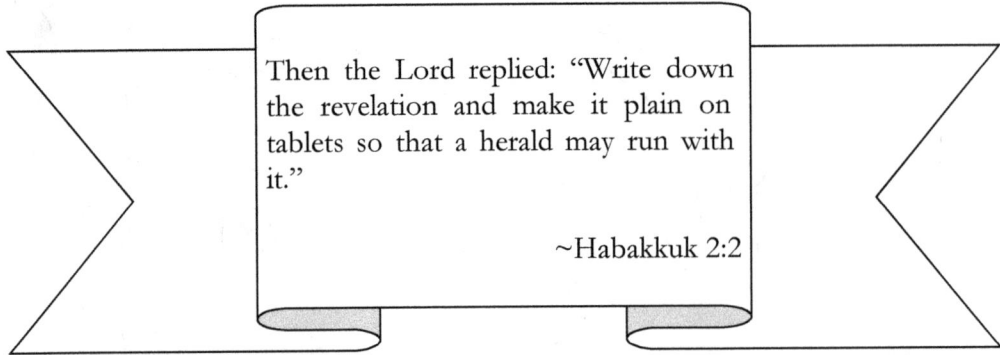

Then the Lord replied: "Write down the revelation and make it plain on tablets so that a herald may run with it."

~Habakkuk 2:2

Christmas Communications

Christmas is a time for communication. We tend to contact people we haven't managed to connect with the entire rest of the year. We send newsletters, greeting cards, and packages. Phone conversations, local coffee shop meetings, visits to friends' homes to admire Christmas decorations and munch homemade cookies all contribute to the holiday festivities.

At least, that's the way it used to be. Now we post pictures of our baked goods and glistening ornaments on Facebook, Instagram, and numero us other social media. We share holiday anecdotes, memories, hopes, and dreams. Thanks to the Internet and social networking, we can communicate with people all over the world from the comfort of our own homes. It's a good thing, right?

Ironically, the use of mass communication can hinder our ability to communicate effectively on a personal level. We seem to be losing our knack as well as our need for face -to-face associations. We are in danger of becoming an isolated society.

We have lost more than we've gained through social networking as far as I'm concerned. To me, nothing says "I love you" like an in-the-flesh visit. You can show me through the Internet pictures of all the cookies you've made. But I can't enjoy them until you place a plateful in my ha nd. Then I can smell the spices, peanut butter, and chocolate. Then and only then, can I dunk one in my coffee and taste the homemade goodness. I'll say it again … nothing beats an in-the-flesh visit.

God knows the importance of hands -on, face-to-face, in-the-flesh communication. That's why He came as a babe. That's why He walked with the people, healed their sick, and washed their feet. That's why He sent His disciples out to minister to the needy. That's why He calls us even today to share His word, His grace, His mercy, His love, and His plan of salvation.

That's why we celebrate Christmas.

Reflections

1. While continuing family traditions of decorating and baking, don't let the tradition of in-the-flesh visits die. Make a list of people with whom you'd like to dunk a cookie in a glass of milk this week, give them a call, and make a date while those cookies are in the oven.

2. We can't visit everyone we love during the Christmas season, but we can make phone calls. Text and instant messages are all right, but nothing beats hearing a loved one's voice on the phone.

3. Greeting cards and newsletters are also getting lost in the Christmas-on-the-Internet shuffle. Nevertheless, plenty of people don't subscribe to the social media madness, especially the elderly. Consider sending cards to those near and far who aren't sailing on cyber-seas.

Prayer

Heavenly Father, although in-the-flesh visiting seems obsolete, it might be fun to dunk some cookies in a glass of milk with my friends and relatives. Help us to put away the Internet long enough to reconnect and enjoy one another this Christmas. In Jesus' name, amen.

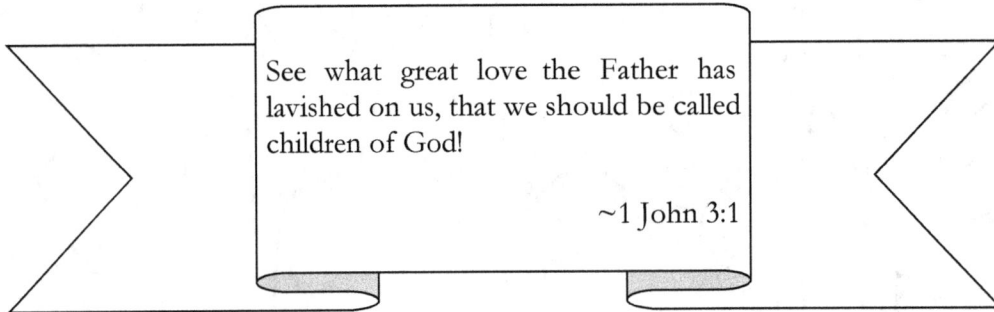

See what great love the Father has lavished on us, that we should be called children of God!

~1 John 3:1

No Greater Love

Christmas is a time of joy and celebration, but not always … not for everyone. Tragedy strikes with no regard to seasons. People are left defenseless, devastated, and hopeless. Since the shooting at the Columbine school several years ago, other irrational individuals have taken the lives of innocent children. In some instances, teachers and principals laid down their lives for the students. The faculty did not deserve to be executed. But love for their pupils compelled them to do whatever necessary to protect the innocent. Although the administrators did as much as possible and paid the ultimate price, they couldn't save all the students. These brave men and women deserve to be commemorated. Their relatives and close friends deserve continued prayer.

Even still due to the increase in such terroristic acts, fear abounds where security once existed. The entire nation lies in shock and in mourning, sickened by the senseless, violent mass murders of elementary school, high school, and college-age students and faculty.

Is it possible an evil force caused these tragedies —the absence of good, the absence of love, the absence of respect for human life?

That evil force always demands the blood of the innocent. However, no blood has ever been spilled as pure and innocent as that of Jesus Christ. Jesus said, "Greater love has no one than this: to lay down one's life for one's friends" (John 15:13). Then He did just that. And His sacrifice has the power to save all who will believe. Unfortunately, not everyone will take Him at His word and trust in Him. However, those who take refuge beneath His wings will be welcomed into His eternal family, not as servants, but as His children. That was His mission during His first advent.

But what about His second coming? During that glorious time, He'll defeat the evil one.

What comfort and joy we derive from knowing Jesus is coming again to restore and heal our land and our broken hearts. So take courage and stand on His promises even when you hurt too much to celebrate.

Reflections

1. Christmas doesn't seem like the time to discuss the evil in the world. We want to concentrate on happy times and lose ourselves in festivities at least for the month of December. Unfortunately, many people don't have that privilege. Today, observe those around you. Are there people close to you who are mourning the loss of a loved one or facing difficult times? How can you lighten their load?

2. Perhaps you are the one shackled by the weight of adverse circumstances this Christmas. Sometimes our sorrow is lifted when we focus on someone else's needs. If one-on-one visits seem too difficult for you right now, try volunteering in a soup kitchen. Or take on a card ministry by sending out a few greeting cards each day to shut-ins.

3. When hardship and heartache deplete our joy, sharing becomes next to impossible. However bad our circumstances may be, we have hope and peace when we celebrate Christmas with Jesus' Second Advent in mind.

Prayer

Heavenly Father, life comes at me strong and wicked like a tsunami at times without checking the calendar for holidays before it hits. Help me to focus on Your everlasting love and on Jesus' second coming. And restore my joy. In Jesus' name, amen.

At that time the kingdom of heaven will be like ten virgins who took their lamps and went out to meet the bridegroom. Five of them were foolish and five were wise. The foolish ones took their lamps but did not take any oil with them. The wise ones, however, took oil in jars along with their lamps.

Matthew 25:1-4

Preparations

Christmas is a time of preparation. Some people start shopping and planning the week after Christmas for the following one. It's a big day in our lives, and we take all precautions to make it as special as possible.

But Christmas isn't the only day of the year that warrants our attention and time. There are birthdays, graduations, summer picnics, Independence Day parades, and vacations to plan. And, of course, the single most important personal event, our weddings.

I began planning my wedding when I was four years old. I had no clue who I'd marry (I didn't meet "Mr. Right" until after I graduated from high school), but I hoped I would get married someday. I played bride with lacy slips and Mom's jewelry. Of course, my tastes changed through the years, which meant my wedding dress wasn't exactly like the one I had played in. However, some things didn't change —like my dream of having an outside wedding.

As much fun as I had preparing for my big day, I wasn't the only one looking ahead to my leaving the proverbial nest. My parents helped me prepare for my departure from the time I was old enough to stand on a chair to dry dishes. Mom taught me to cook, clean, take pride in personal hygiene, and to seek God above all things. Meanwhile, Daddy taught me to stand on moral principles, to never make promises I didn't intend to keep, and to pray with all my heart. They shaped me into a woman capable of taking care of herself yet submissive enough to bring honor to her husband as well as to her God.

Now my wedding day is a forty-year-old memory. In retrospect, I realize it too was nothing more than preparation for an even grander event … the marriage of the Bride Groom of heaven to His Bride, the church, of which I am a member. Think of the most elaborate, exquisite wedding celebration you've ever heard of, and you'll only be touching the hem of the church's bridal gown.

Reflections

1. What if we spent as much time preparing for Jesus' wedding day as we spend on Christmas Day? Time's a wasting. To whom can you extend an invitation?

2. Weddings unite families and often restore broken relationships. How can you offer yourself as an agent through whom God can restore a relationship?

3. What else can you do in preparation for Jesus' return?

Prayer

Heavenly Father, the day of celebration fast approaches, and I fear I'll be among those who lack "oil for their lamps." Show me what I need to do to prepare for Your wedding feast. And help me encourage others to do the same. In Jesus' name, amen.

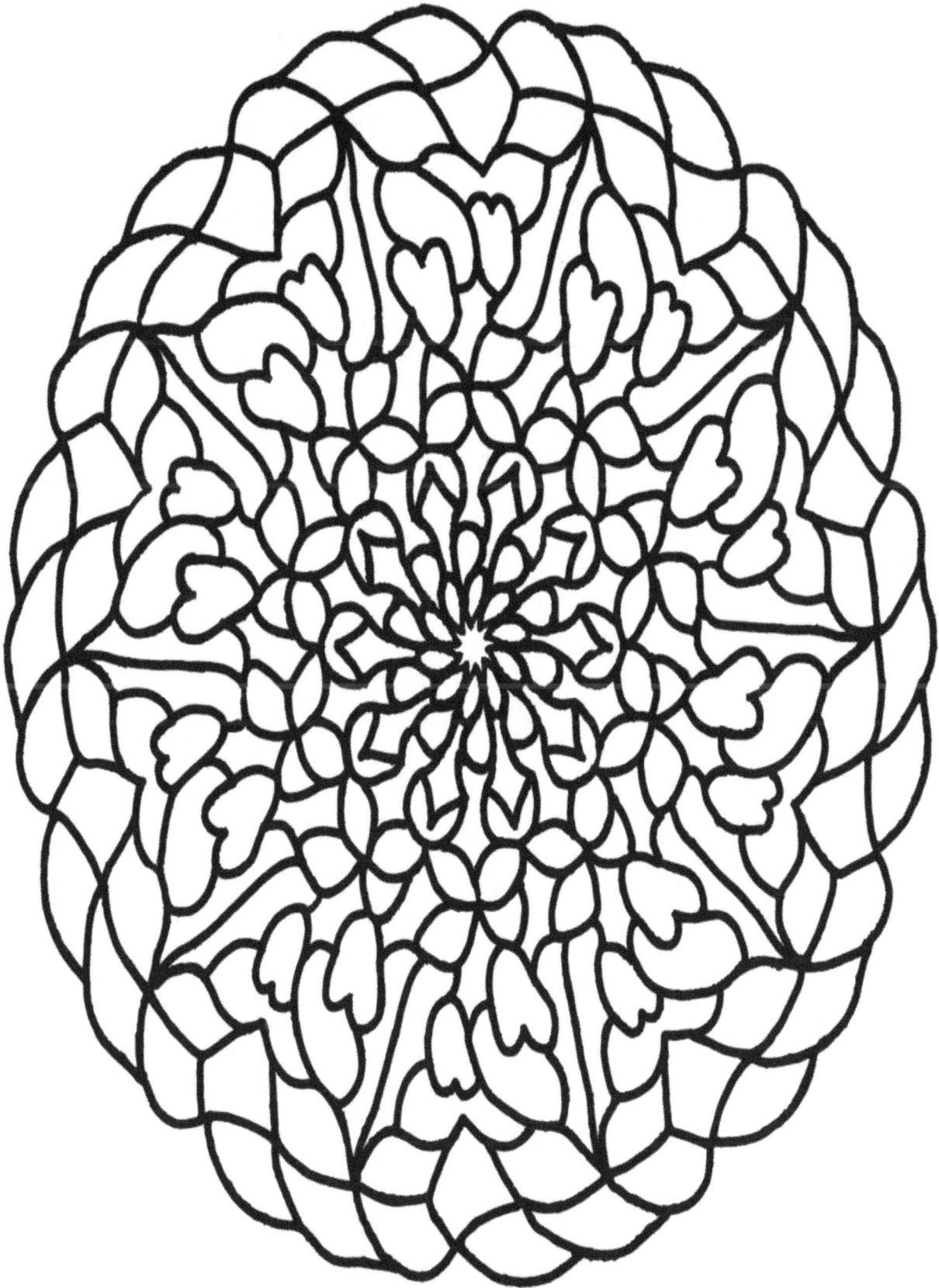

Is not this the kind of fasting I have chosen: to loose the chains of injustice and untie the cords of the yoke, to set the oppressed free and break every yoke? Is it not to share your food with the hungry and to provide the poor wanderer with shelter—when you see the naked, to clothe them, and not to turn away from your own flesh and blood?

~Isaiah 58:6-7

A Christmas Fast

Twas two days after Christmas when all through the house

Everybody was overfed including the mouse;

All the toys lay broken, tossed on a pile.

The children sat in a row, none with a smile

While they insisted on getting more stuff,

Mother slammed the bedroom door in a huff.

The children continued to cry and to pout

Until Father ended it with a thunderous shout.

"This isn't what Christmas is meant to be.

It isn't about you, your Mother, or me.

It's all about giving, yes, indeed;

It's all about giving to those in need;

It's about Jesus who gave His life on a cross

To give eternal hope to those who are lost.

It's about giving of ourselves, His story to share

And helping one another our burdens to bear."

Tears streaming and gleaming on their sorry faces,

The children jumped down from their lofty places,

They gathered their toys and began to mend;

Soon the playthings were like new again.

The children wrapped their toys and kept not a one;

Giving to needy kids proved much more fun,

The family learned a lesson in fasting that day

God is delighted when we give things away.

When we deprive ourselves of things we need,

It should be for the sake of doing a good deed.

If you show kindness to others keep it hush-hush;

When you see Jesus, there'll be no reason to blush.

He'll say, "Well done my good and faithful friend,"

And you'll receive blessings upon blessings in the end.

Reflections

1. We seldom think of fasting during Christmastime. It's a time of celebrating, which includes overeating and overindulging on many levels. Nevertheless, fasting cleanses the body and the soul, and today offers an excellent time to fast. Step back from all the busyness of the season and all of the indulgences. Reflect on the true meaning of Christmas, all your blessings, and the needs of others.

2. Fasting offers time to draw close to God, to fellowship with Him on a higher level. What better time to seek Him than the time of year in which we celebrate His advent?

3. Fasting, although usually associated with food, involves doing without something important to us … a sacrifice. A sacrifice benefits no one unless someone else receives something of equal or greater value. Consider the cost of the meal or item you plan to go without. To whom could you give an equally valued item?

Prayer

Heavenly Father, I've never thought about fasting for Christmas before. What can I give back to You this Christmas to benefit someone else and to draw closer to You? In Jesus' name, amen.

Then he went down to Nazareth with them and was obedient to them. But his mother treasured all these things in her heart. And Jesus grew in wisdom and stature, and in favor with God and man.

~Luke 2:51-52

Obedience

With little thought about the lessons of obedience they enforced, our parents steered us from harmful situations as we scurried on hands and knees across the floor. They continued with their training as we progressed through the toddler years, re-enforcing rules and preparing us for school.

Teachers then joined in the development of our obedience a nd respect for authority by giving homework assignments and conjuring up exams.

By the time we reached adulthood, most of us understood the importance of following rules and the necessity of accountability. We also knew people in authority had the right to demand proper conduct from us and enforce consequences if we chose not to comply with the rules.

As our example, Jesus entered our world as a baby in compliance to His Heavenly Father's plan. Jesus didn't leap from the babe in the manger to the Miracle Man walking the dusty streets of Israel. First, He learned to obey His earthly father. Joseph taught Jesus carpentry, Jewish customs, and the laws of Moses. Thereby, Jesus grew in wisdom and stature, and in favor with God and man (Luke 2:52) in much the same way the rest of us have matured.

By the time Jesus was twelve years old, He knew the importance of God 's law and stumped the scholars of His day (Luke 2:41:49). Although He had the desire to be about His Father's business and to teach the true word of God, He understood the necessity of obeying His earthly father. Jesus returned home with Joseph and remained there until He entered His ministry. Then He spoke often about the importance of obeying the Father. Jesus said, "Anyone who loves me will obey my teachings" (John 14:23).

Reflections

1. Components, such as fear, respect, and the promise of rewards, often encourage obedience, but nothing delights God more than obedience through love. Check your motives for obedience. If you follow the rules for other reasons, how can you turn your submissive behavior into an act of love for God?

2. Jesus entered our world as a baby, becoming subject to the laws of those He created. What does that teach you about obedience through love?

3. I'm discovering as I celebrate Christmas through obedience to God's instruction, "So whether you eat or drink or whatever you do, do it all for the glory of God" (1 Corinthians 10:31), the entire holiday season has become less stressful … relaxing even. Work on putting Jesus in the center of your activities and see what happens.

Prayer:

Heavenly Father, often I seem to do all the right things for all the wrong reasons unlike Jesus. He came out of love for You and for me. He remained focused on His mission, driven by that love. Because I want to be like Him and want to express my love to You, I set aside all my selfish motives and determine to bring you honor through my actions. In Jesus' name, amen.

Love [that is, unselfishly seek the best or higher good for] your enemies, and do good, and lend, expecting nothing in return; for your reward will be great (rich, abundant), and you will be sons of the Most High; because He Himself is kind and gracious and good to the ungrateful and the wicked.

~Luke 6:35 AMP

Expectations

While cookie baking, gift making, and rug shaking, I daydream of the upcoming events. I admit the expectations at our house soar higher with each chore we cross off our to-do lists. My husband and I expect our daughters home for the holidays, accompanied by their husbands and chi ldren. They expect their favorite foods. We expect them to replace the lids on cookie jars, sweep up the crumbs, and do the dishes. They expect some items on their wish list to appear under the tree. In return, we expect a little gratitude. We all expect hugs, kisses, and lots of laughter.

Nevertheless, our expectations, at times, become as disheveled as the living room while little ones rip open their gifts. Such was Gene's and my first Christmas together. One month after our wedding, Uncle Sam decided we needed a three-month separation. So, the United States Army flew Gene across the continent to California for boot camp.

A week before Christmas, the army shipped him home—wonderful present for the two of us. Gene expected me to arrive at the airport with bells on . . . it was Christmas after all. I expected to look my best. He expected me to be there waiting on him. I expected him to wait patiently on me. He expected me to, at least, be on time. I expected him to forgive my tardiness. Although the hour he spent alone at the airport seemed like a month of Mondays, Gene expected me to show up … eventually. I expected him to greet me with a bear hug, which he did. And I returned it. Perhaps part of the joy was the spirit of expectancy that stirred in our hearts through those moments of waiting.

Reflections

1. Christmas stirs the same spirit of expectancy in our hearts with gifts and visits and memories. However, it may be wise to keep our expectations at bay to avoid disappointment.

2. As we cultivate the spirit of expectancy for the big day, we may find some people fail to meet our expectations. Let's face it, we often fall short of their expectations as well. Let's practice forgiveness and enjoy the day for what it is—a celebration of Jesus' coming.

3. Expectations contribute to the joy as well as the stress of the day as we anticipate the upcoming events. Nevertheless, the Father never said to commemorate the birth of His Son, instead, He emphatically commands us to encourage one another with the blessed assurance of His return. Can you imagine? As spectacular as Jesus' first advent must have been, it's only a foreshadowing of what is to come. Go ahead, unleash your expectations about His second coming. Jesus will meet them all above and beyond your wildest imaginations.

Prayer

Heavenly Father, expectations sure can put a damper on holiday festivities. Help me to stay focused on You, who cannot fail. In Jesus' name, amen.

Whoever wants to become great among you must be your servant, and whoever wants to be first must be your slave—just as the Son of Man did not come to be served, but to serve, and to give his life as a ransom for many.

~Matthew 20:26-28

Service for the King

Several years ago, my daughter Rachel gave me one of the best gifts ever. She had taken the time to create a coupon book filled with offers of things I enjoy doing—things like a movie night for just the two of us, dinner at her house, and a book review (what writer wouldn't appreciate that?). It cost her very little. But I cherished her thoughtfulness. Although the coupons remain intact, tucked away in my dresser drawer for sweet memories sake, that book delights me every time I look at it. Her gift serves as a reminder of wha t true Christmas giving is all about.

Christmas giving isn't about receiving. It isn't even about giving. It is all about serving.

The difference between giving and serving is as great as the difference between giving and receiving. Yet a fine line separates the two concepts. To many, giving simply means transferring material stuff from one person to another. It can come from the heart and be very meaningful. Nevertheless, the act of giving in this respect falls short of the image Jesus presents through His talk with the disciples as He stood a child in their midst and said, "Whoever welcomes one of these little children in my name welcomes me; and whoever welcomes me does not welcome me but the one who sent me" (Mark 9:37). Perhaps, Jesus used a child to illustrate His desire and concern for service because there is no one so needy as a young child. They have no capability of self-care but must rely on someone else to supply their needs.

Tending to the necessities of small children is a service that Jesus held in high regard. But He never wanted it to end there. We are to consider other's needs, adults as well as children, more important than our own. Finding ways of helping others, even if they are capable of doing for themselves, shows love on a higher level than the mere transferring of stuff.

Jesus came to earth as the servant to all humanity. He taught and lived servitude. He still does. And He expects it from His followers. While on earth, Jesus served others by healing the sick, feeding the hungry, raising the dead, and ultimately taking our sins upon Himself on the cross. He did for us what we could not do for ourselves.

Reflections

1. Make a coupon book filled with offers of service and give it to someone who typically serves you … like your hairstylist, your pet groomer, or your local waitstaff. Who else serves you that you'd like to favor with a service?

2. Service is a voluntary act that benefits the recipient with no expectations of payment or awards. If you live in an area where you get snow, clear your neighbor's driveway or walkway without telling them.

3. Take a lesson from the current fad called "Pay it Forward" and pay the bill for someone you don't know the next time you go to a restaurant.

Prayer

Heavenly Father, I want to follow Jesus' example and cultivate a servant-like attitude within me. Show me ways to serve others this Christmas and throughout the coming year. In Jesus' name, amen.

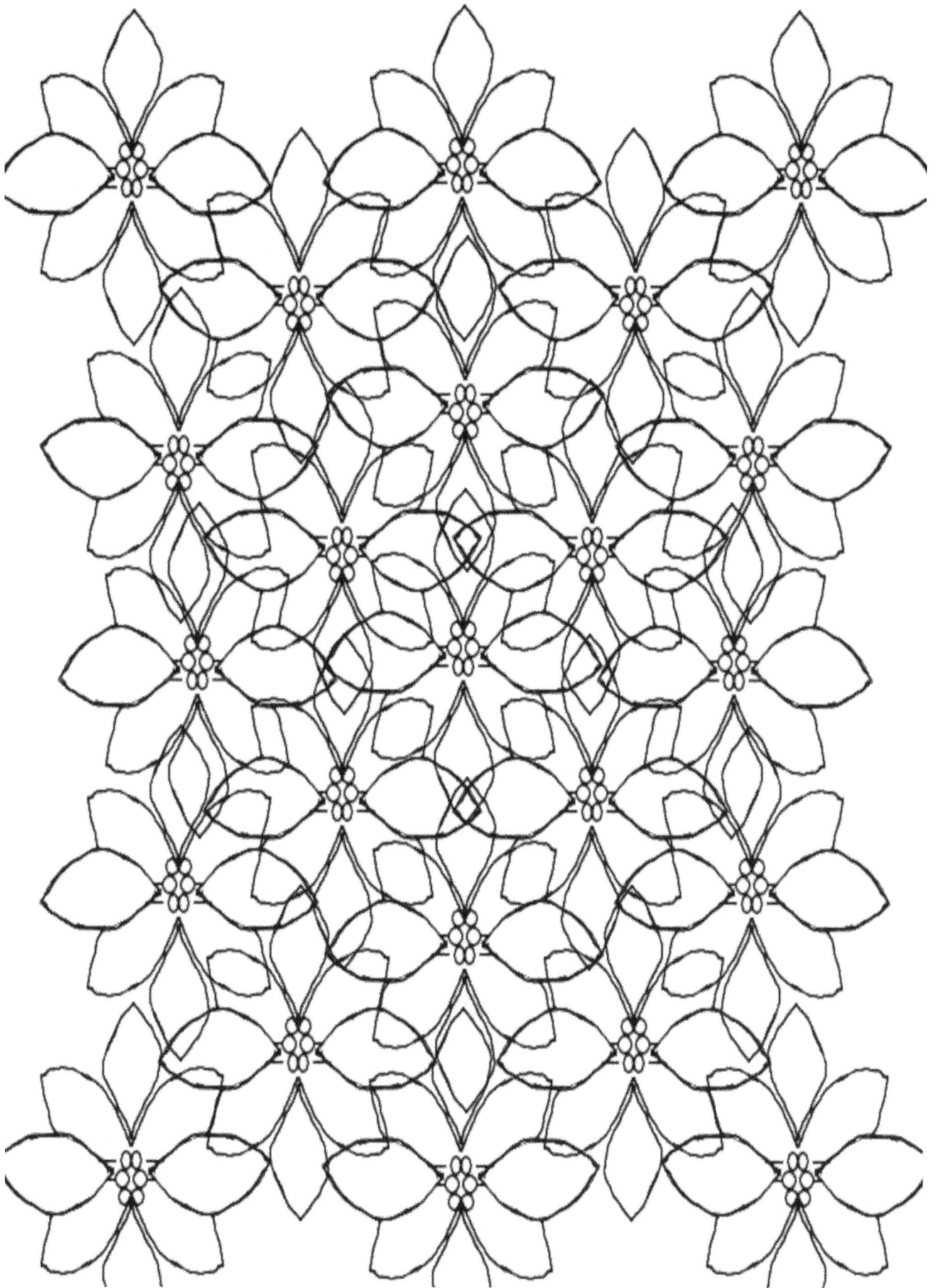

I wait for the Lord, my whole being waits, and in his word I put my hope. I wait for the Lord more than watchmen wait for the morning: I say, more than watchmen wait for the morning.

~Psalms 130:5-6

Motivation

"Brenda wake up. It's Christmas!" My older brother's enthusiasm whirled in my ears and lifted me to my feet.

Eddie always woke first on Christmas morning—4:30 a.m—without fail. Once he claimed jingling, sleigh bells aroused him. I believed his story, and the excitement of the day stirred in me as we tiptoed down the steps. We stopped on the landing of the two sets of stairs. One set led to the kitchen. The other, an open staircase, stretched out into the front room where the Christmas tree guarded our presents. We sat on the top step and feasted on the eye-candy, filling our minds with wonder. When we absorbed all we could handle, we ran back upstairs to wake our sisters. Then the four of us repeated the routine.

Obeying the rule, no waking parents before 6:00 a.m., felt like cruel and unusual punishment. Tick-tock, tick-tock, the clock droned as though its sole desire was to torture us. Finally, the big hand stood on the little hand's head, and eight feet stampeded into our parents' bedroom.

Every year my brother's Christmas-morning enthusiasm captivated and motivated our entire family to get up and begin the festivities. Eddie never lost hope of receiving everything he wanted.

If we look forward to receiving everything God has for us according to His word, enthusiasm will fill our souls like Christmas filled my brother's mind with excitement. Based on God's infallible promises, our enthusiasm should ignite genuine hope in others, which will motivate them to begin walking in the light of the Lord.

Yet our expectations are too shallow. We can't dream big enough to envision the wonders God is preparing for those who love Him. The grandest festivities on earth will appear as dust particles dancing in the sunlight when compared to the second coming of Jesus Christ.

Nonetheless, hope has a tendency to diminish as the second hand ticks around the clock. I stand motionless watching, listening to the endless tick-tock of my inner clock reminding me of the brevity of life. I wonder if Jesus' Second Advent will ever arrive. I wrestle with the temptation to fall asleep. Instead of waking others, I need someone to wake me and infuse me with enthusiasm like my brother used to do.

Reflections

1. That's why we celebrate Christmas—to keep us motivated. The excitement of the appearance of the Christ child stirs anticipation of His second coming within us. How can you encourage someone to wait on the Lord's Second Advent?

2. Take a few moments to reflect on Christmases past. What filled your mind with wonder and excitement as a child? What fills your mind with wonder and excitement now?

3. I don't know about you, but I have lost much of my childhood Christmas enthusiasm. The wonder of the season has diminished. But I'm working on restoring it by concentrating more on the events that took place during Jesus' birth. If you've lost some of your wonderment too, what can you do to revive it?

Prayer

Heavenly Father, Christmases past serve as reminders of what was and what is to come. Thank You for sweet memories and the assurance of a far greater celebration. In Jesus' name, amen.

Let each one give [thoughtfully and with purpose] just as he has decided in his heart, not grudgingly or under compulsion, for God loves a cheerful giver [and delights in the one whose heart is in his gift].

~2 Corinthians 9:7 AMP

Christmas Ought to Be ...

Cheerful ...   The number of fancy-wrapped boxes tied with red ribbons under a tree Christmas morning adds little cheer. The people giving and receiving the boxes bring cheer to the scene tucked within their hearts

Humorous ... Mugs of hot chocolate embellished with trays of cut-out cookies tickle our taste buds while humorous stories replenish our overstressed souls.

Reminiscent ... Memories twirl through our heads—the cherished, the longed-for, the woeful—shaping our take on Christmas. But each year offers opportunities to reshape Christmas into what it ought to be.

Inspirational ... Tales of angels, shepherds, a maiden, and the Christ -child—a gift to us all—inspire us to trust God without question, to live within His promises, and to seek His face.

Special ...   Family and friends gathered together add pizazz to the season from Thanksgiving Day to Christmas Day. Warm hugs, understanding smiles, and lots and lots of laughter make any day special, but those shared during the holidays bring unique comfort and healing to hurting souls.

Traditional ... Christmases past, like presents opened with care and gratitude, radiate with a sense of belonging and emit a sense of security we all need . Traditions can transcend generations or be something exclusive to our immediate family. Regardless of the time span, they bind us together.

Manageable ... With our long to-do lists, Christmas easily spins out of control. But we can make it manageable through the process of elimination. If something causes stress and can be avoided, cross it off the list.

Adventurous ... While traditions bind us together, new schemes and themes add luster, rekindle enthusiasm, and can reestablish the true meaning of Christmas.

Shared ...   The gospel of Jesus Christ, the recitals, the songs, the prayers, the gifts, the food, the memories—all of it is meant to be shared with those around us.

Reflections

1. Christmas Day has arrived. Share a platter of cheer garnished with humor and a side dish of tradition sprinkled with memories.

2. Drink from the cup of adventure sweetened with inspiration.

3. Savor the fragrance of joy, love, and laughter.

Prayer:

Heavenly Father, the day of celebration has arrived. As we share the blessings of family and friends, remind us to honor and glorify Jesus throughout the day. In His name, amen.

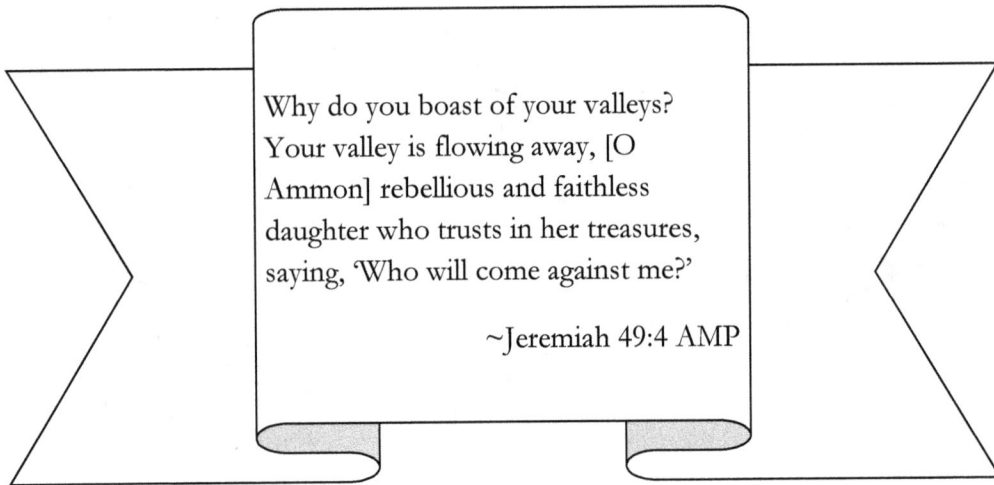

Why do you boast of your valleys? Your valley is flowing away, [O Ammon] rebellious and faithless daughter who trusts in her treasures, saying, 'Who will come against me?'

~Jeremiah 49:4 AMP

Lacy Bohnes' Christmas Wish (Part 1)

Queen Aikee sat on the floor—her dress tattered and hair a sight. Princess Lacy Bohnes stood with arms folded and her tiny face twisted in a defiant knot. Broken toys cluttered the room.

"I want Christmas now!" demanded the child.

"But Christmas isn't until the week after next, darling." The queen reached for her daughter. But Lacy stepped backward.

"I want it now!"

"I cannot change time, Lacy. And you are acting like a three-year old. You're twelve and know you don't get everything you want. I just don't understand how you became so self-centered. Your father and I have tried our best not to spoil you. But the harder we try, the worse you become."

The door creaked open. At the sight of the butler and a woman, the queen jumped to her feet and straightened her dress, obviously in the most dignified manner she could muster. "Wherever did you come from?"

"Sorry for the intrusion, Your Highness." The butler bowed. "I brought a ... a Christmas miracle, if you will." He pointed to the woman.

She curtsied as was expected from royal subjects, although she wasn't one. "Misty Meanor at your service. You may call me Misty."

Lacy scowled at the woman.

The queen's eyes widened. Her face flushed. "Oh you are a Christmas miracle indeed. We thought we had exhausted all the nannies available in the kingdom. Please, come meet your new charge, my sweet daughter Lacy."

"Good day, Lacy." Misty greeted her with the same curtsy.

Lacy's scowl grew into a scornful huff. "Did you bring Christmas?"

"Child, your mother is correct. She, nor I, nor anyone can change time. Christmas will come on its appointed day."

Lacy stomped her foot and pitched another china doll to the floor, shattering its delicate form into a hundred pieces. "I want new toys now."

Misty smiled wryly and turned to the queen. "Your Highness, I need time alone with your daughter if I am to do my job properly."

"Ah, yes ... of course." The queen ambled to Lacy and kissed her cheek. Lacy wiped it off. "Be sweet, my baby girl."

With that, Queen Aikee strolled to the butler's side. He bowed and extended his arm as he opened the door. The queen proceeded into the corridor. The butler followed, shutting the door behind them.

"So," said the woman to the girl, "you want what you want when you want it ... even Christmas."

"Yes," Princess Lacy pursed her lips.

Misty's smile stretched into a broad grin. "As I said, I cannot change time. But I can help you get everything you want when you want it."

"You can?" The princess let down her guard and smiled back. "How?"

"I have a potion … but you must follow the instructions with great care. If you miss a step or pu t them in the wrong order, you will surely lose all that you have and lose all favor with your father forever."

"Misty Meanor, I suspect you may be a witch."

"Ha! Do you indeed, child?" Misty laughed again. "Do you, indeed?"

"If so, you must have an ulterior motive. What do you gain by giving me this potion? What is your price?"

(Read Part 2 of Lacy Bohnes' Christmas Wish in tomorrow's devotion)

Reflections:

1. Temper tantrums are unbecoming of princesses as well as of you and me. Yet Yuletide -stress can cause our tempers to flare. *We* might even throw our china dolls. What can you do to quench the fire before your temper explodes?

2. Alone-time relieves stress. How about a bubble bath, a short walk, or a cup of tea and a good book?

3. Are you expecting too much from yourself and others at Christmastime? What can you let go of to have a more enjoyable holiday?

Prayer:

Heavenly Father, before I act like a spoiled princess and do something I'll regret like smashing my favorite china doll, put Your peace in my heart. Remind me to take time out for You. In Jesus' name, amen.

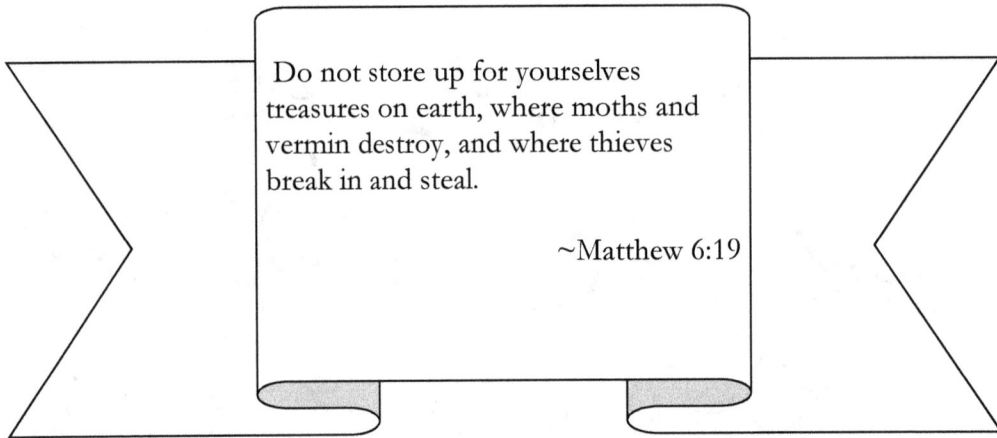

Do not store up for yourselves treasures on earth, where moths and vermin destroy, and where thieves break in and steal.

~Matthew 6:19

Lacy Bohnes' Christmas Wish (Part 2)

As the first rays of the morning sun glimmered through the palace windows, Lacy waltzed down the corridor into the kitchen. She brewed a cup of tea to Misty's specifications, following the instructions precisely.

Misty Meanor promised Father would become most agreeable after just one sip of this potion, Lacy mused. *I shall have Christmas now and everything I've always wanted, but was denied.* With cup and saucer in hand, she ambled into the royal dining hall where her father and mother sat nibbling on breakfast biscuits.

"Ah, there you are, my princess." King Justice motioned for his daughter to join them.

Lacy curtsied before the king. "I've brought your morning tea as usual, Father." She handed him the cup.

"You are a princess fair, my child." The queen smiled. "Come, sit. Cook has prepared your favorite breakfast—peanut butter chocolate chip muffins."

While Lacy enjoyed her muffins, the king sipped his tea. "This is the finest brew ever."

Lacy smiled. "You always say that, Father."

"So I do. But today I'm feeling particularly generous. What would my daughter desire from her king?"

"Why, all the toys in the land, of course." Lacy said without hesitation.

"But Christmas is coming, dear child," Father said. "If you get everything today, what will we give you then?"

"You're the king. You'll think of something." Lacy grinned.

"Well said." Father nodded. "You shall have your wish today."

Mother's eyes widened. "What? We had agreed, my king, that our daughter shall not receive everything her heart desires. For such luxuries only serve to spoil the child and never impart the wisdom needed to govern oneself, let alone a kingdom."

King Justice glanced at his wife then refocused on Lacy. "Never mind all that, my queen. I have given my word and will not revoke it."

The king kept his word, and for the next two weeks, caravans of merchants streamed nonstop through the palace gates, stuffing every nook and cranny of the palace, the courtyard, and even the royal stables with toys.

Christmas morning, Lacy stormed into the dining hall without her father's tea. "Father, there are no ..." She stopped in her tracks before her mother. "Where is he?"

"He's gone."

"Gone? He can't be gone. It's Christmas morning. And there are no presents under the tree."

"He has gone to find—"

"More toys, of course. They stopped coming two days ago."

"No. He has gone to find the true princess. We fear there may have b een a switch at birth. And perhaps dear child, you are not our daughter."

(Read Part 3 of Lacy Bohnes' Christmas Wish in tomorrow's devotion)

Reflections

1. After all the preparations, the gifts opened, the meal eaten, many of us experience an emotional crash. I've found hiding one gift for the end of the day and making up a riddle for the recipient to solve in order to find the gift helps soften the letdown. What can you do to ease the emotional crash?

2. Singing sooths the achy soul. Dig out some of your favorite praise songs and have a sing-along with family and friends.

3. How about coloring? Nothing relieves stress or eases letdowns like coloring with a child.

Prayer

Heavenly Father, show me ways to honor You in both the highs and lows of Christmas. In Jesus' name, amen.

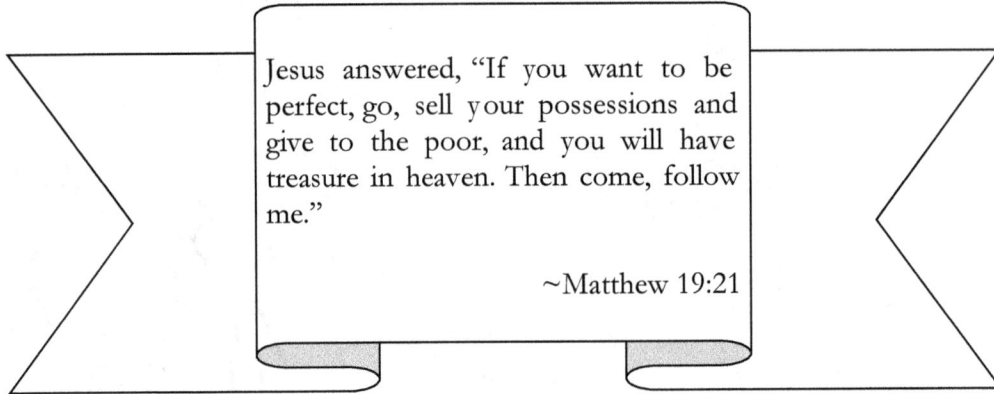

Jesus answered, "If you want to be perfect, go, sell your possessions and give to the poor, and you will have treasure in heaven. Then come, follow me."

~Matthew 19:21

Lacy Bohnes' Christmas Wish (Part 3)

"How absurd! Of course I'm your daughter. Look at me." Lacy leaned in nose-to-nose with her mother. "I have my father's eyes and your petite nose and bright smile. Everyone says so."

"Looks do not a princess make. What's in her heart constitutes a true heir to the throne. No real princess could or should be so full of greed and selfishness as you are. We've suspected this terrible fate for some time. But could not bring ourselves to face the truth. We hoped as you grew older your disposition would change. Even with our prodding and pleading you've become more selfish. We cannot possibly bequeath our kingdom to such a person. An heir to our throne must consider the necessities of our royal subjects above her own desires."

"Stop. I want Father. He will see that I am your daughter. When will he be home?"

"Perhaps never. If, indeed, there has been a switch, his quest shall be very dangerous." The queen dabbed at her tears with one of the king's embroidered handkerchiefs. "Now go to your chambers at once. I cannot tolerate the selfish girl you've become."

"Mother, please." Lacy dropped to her knees before the queen. "Don't cast me out of the palace."

"I will do no such thing, child, for only you can save your father from the peril he now faces."

"I'll do whatever you ask. I just want Father back."

"If you truly want him back because you love him and not because of all he can give you, you must seek the antidote from Misty, the witch who gave you the potion that cast the toy curse on our family and our kingdom. You'll find her in the dungeon."

"In the dungeon? So that's where Nanny's been for the past fortnight."

"Yes, I placed her there myself the day your father drank ..."

Lacy ran from her mother straight to the dungeon, sneaked passed the guards, and crept into the witch's cell.

"You have come to release me?" whispered the crone.

"I've come to ask for the formula to break the curse you have placed on my father and me."

"I have done nothing except give you an alternative, child. You're selfishness put the curse in place, casting you and me into a prison from which we cannot escape."

"But I didn't know about such a curse. I only wanted what I wanted now." Lacy wept bitter tears of remorse. "My greed is evil, but I want to change. I want to free us both and find my father before disaster befalls him. Mother says I can prove my worthiness. But only you have the answer."

"Compassion, child. Compassion holds the key."

"Compassion?"

"Yes. Do you love your father enough to show compassion to the poor? Are you willing to give away everything you have to ensure your father's safe return?"

Lacy widened her eyes. "Everything? Even my china dolls?"

"Everything, especially your china dolls, right down to the floor where your broken toys lie."

"I shall do it to save Father."

(Read Part 4 of Lacy Bohnes' Christmas Wish in tomorrow's devotion)

Reflections

1. Teaching children compassion takes time. So the sooner we start the better.

2. Encourage the youngsters in your life to give away like-new toys and clothes. If possible, take the children to a shelter to make the donations themselves.

3. Children learn best by example. How can you show compassion to a child?

Prayer

Heavenly Father, You give with compassion. Me? I'm not so good at it. But I'm willing to learn for Jesus' sake. In His name I pray, amen.

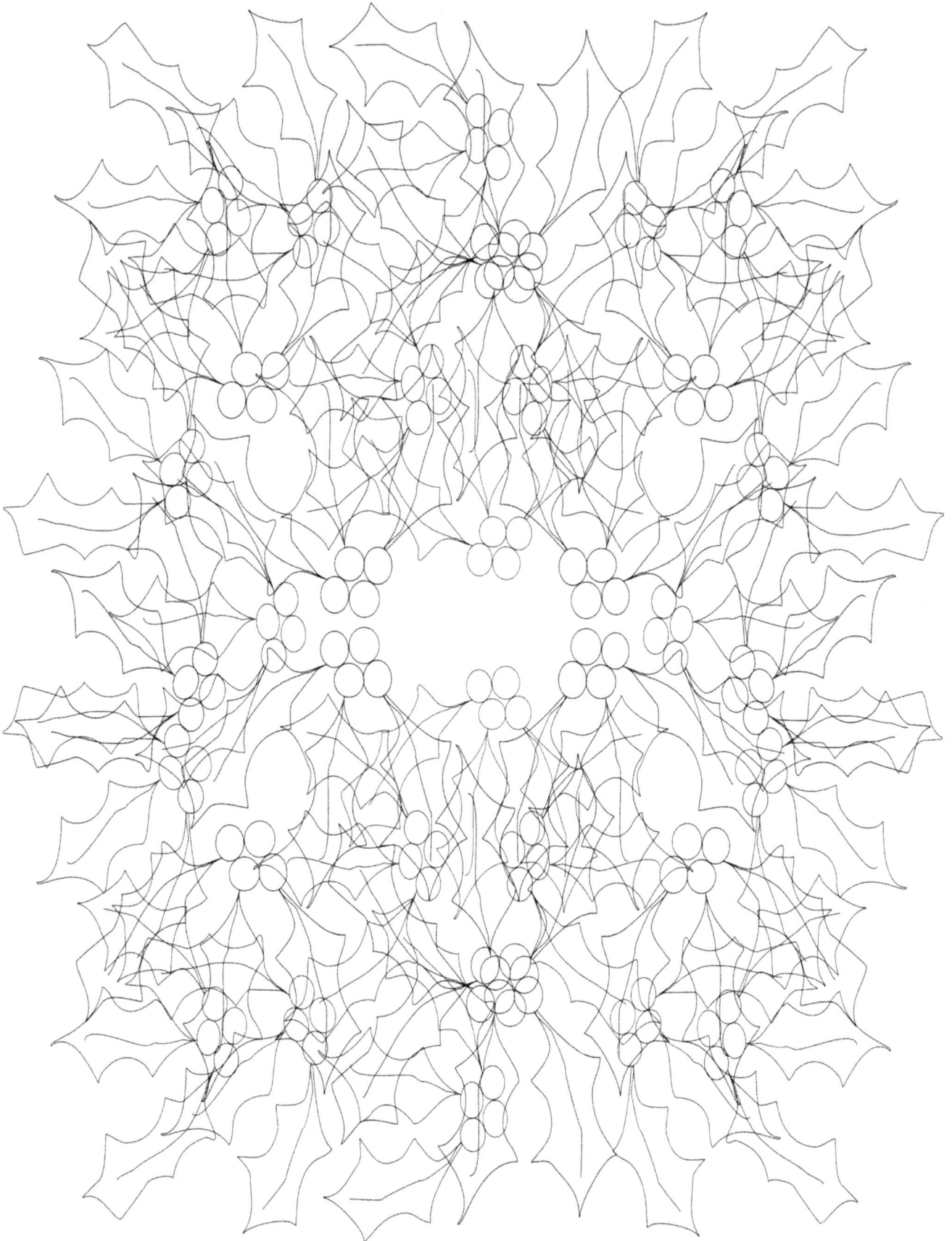

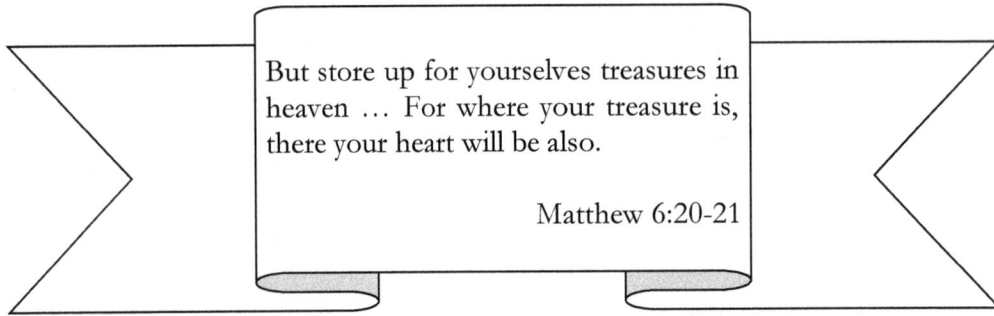

But store up for yourselves treasures in heaven … For where your treasure is, there your heart will be also.

Matthew 6:20-21

Lacy Bohnes' Christmas Wish (Part 4)

Lacy's heart sank as she packed the first cart full of her precious toys. She climbed into the driver's seat and snapped the reigns. "Get moving, Fury. We have a lot of work to do."

The stallion galloped into the nearest town. Lacy halted him at the first house, slipped off the cart, and knocked on the door. When the door cracked, she said, "Are there any children about?"

A little girl in a plain dress opened the door wide. "Yeth, I'm a children."

Lacy giggled. "I have a present for you and all the children in your house and all the children in the whole town."

"Are you a Christmath angel? 'Cause Poppa said unleth a Christmath angel comes there'll be no Christmath in all the kingdom. The greedy princeth demanded all the toyth in the kingdom be delivered to the palath."

Lacy choked back her tears. She hadn't realized her self-centeredness robbed all the children in the kingdom of Christmas.

"I'm not a Christmas angel. But I have lots of toys." Lacy motioned to her cart. "Come. You can have your pick of china dolls."

The little girl squealed with delight. She chose the doll clothed in a white, fine-silk dress trimmed in red lace. It had been Lacy's favorite. But the joy on the child's face as she cradled the doll in her arms put a crack in Lacy's greedy heart. An ounce of compassion leaked out.

With each passing day and every toy give-a-way, self-centeredness yielded to compassion and joy, neither of which had Lacy ever experienced before.

On returning to the palace with her last empty cart, Lacy realized a year had passed and tomorrow Christmas would arrive on its appointed day. She unhitched the horses and went straightaway to her chambers. In her bedroom—devoid of all toys—Lacy sat on her bed, pondering the events of the past year and the joy she had gained from giving. How she wanted to give something special to her mother. But, she had nothing left … nothing to soothe the queen in her grief for the missing king. Even the broken toys Lacy had ordered mended and given to needy children. But there remained one in a box the craftsman insisted was too broken to restore.

Lacy pulled the box out from its hiding place under her bed, hugged it, and lay beside it. She snuggled the box until she drifted off to sleep.

(Read the conclusion of Lacy Bohnes' Christmas Wish in tomorrow's devotion)

Reflections:

1. The act of giving is a gift to the giver. What reactions to gifts you've given do you treasure most this Christmas?

2. If you haven't done it yet, visit a shut-in. Take some baked goods, a small gift, or better yet a child. You'll be surprised the blessing you'll receive.

3. Name some blessing you received from giving this year.

Prayer:

Heavenly Father, thank You for the ability and the opportunities You have given me to give not only to those I love, but to those I don't even know. In Jesus' name, amen.

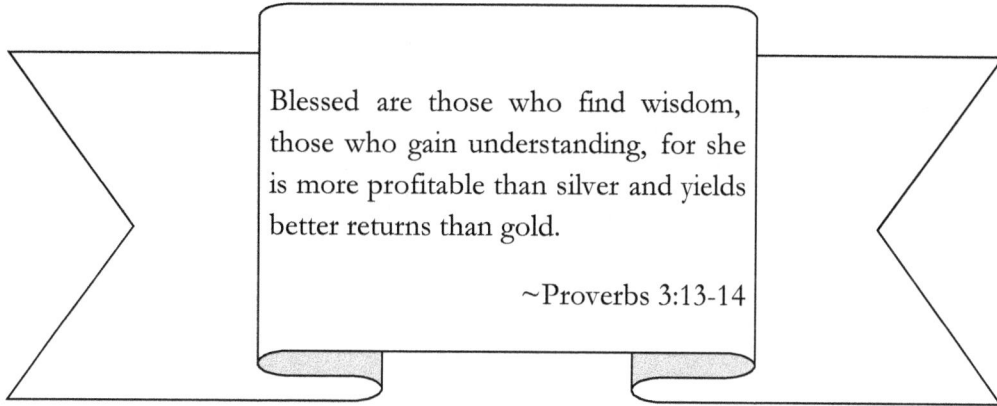

Blessed are those who find wisdom, those who gain understanding, for she is more profitable than silver and yields better returns than gold.

~Proverbs 3:13-14

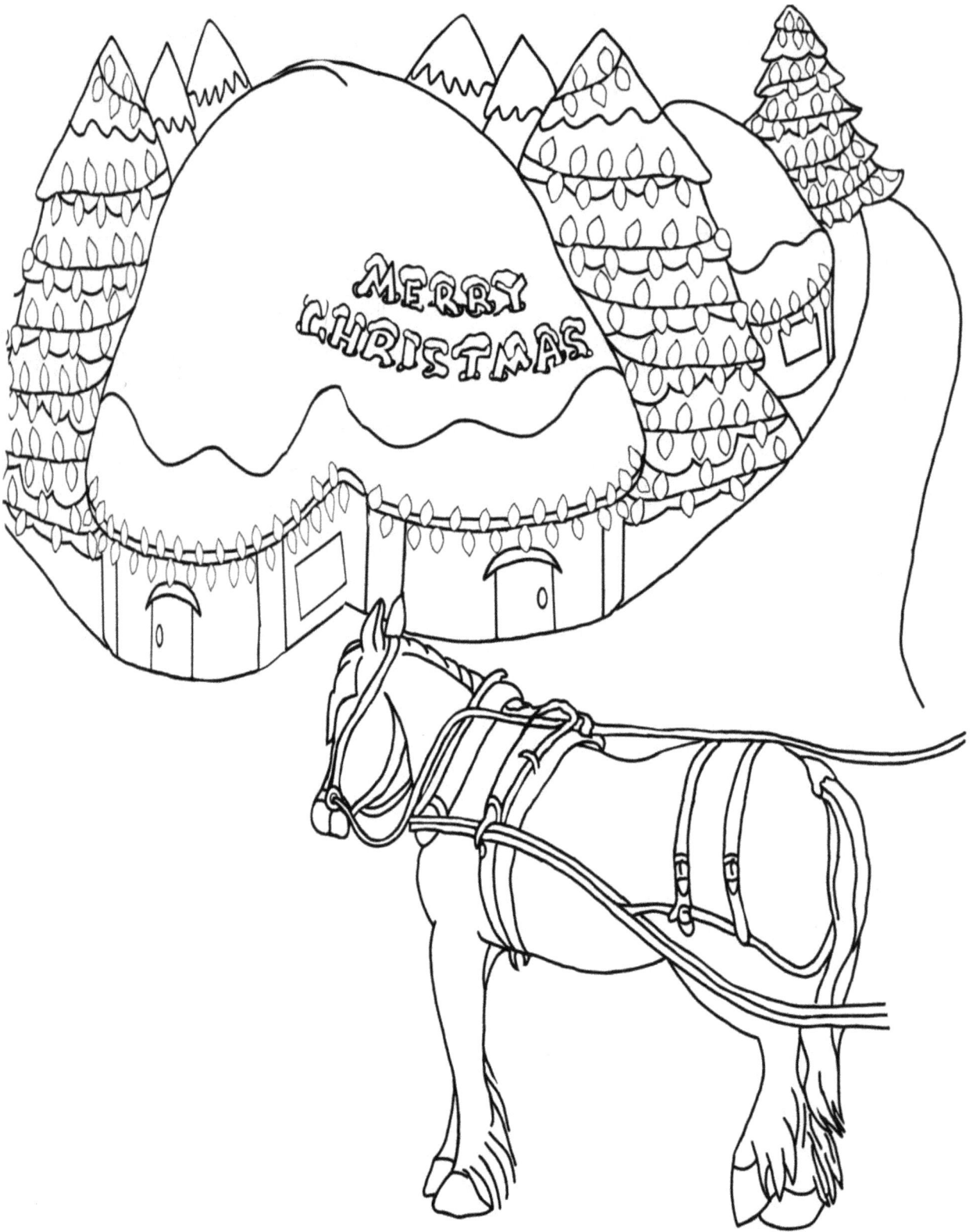

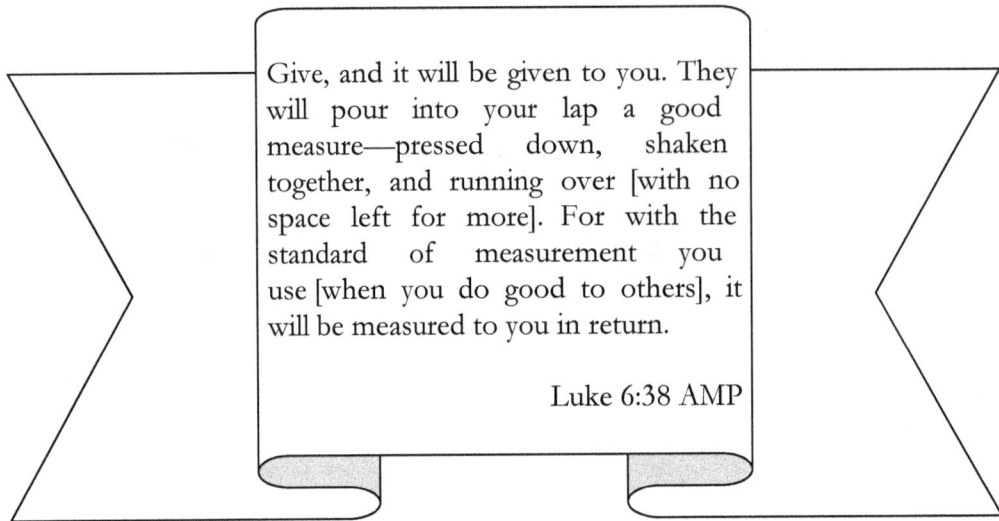

Give, and it will be given to you. They will pour into your lap a good measure—pressed down, shaken together, and running over [with no space left for more]. For with the standard of measurement you use [when you do good to others], it will be measured to you in return.

Luke 6:38 AMP

Lacy Bohnes' Christmas Wish (Part 5)

Long before dawn, Lacy woke with an idea. She found some glue in a drawer, opened the box, and began the tedious repair work. She put the last piece in place as the first rays of the morning sun sparkled through her window. She returned the toy to the box, closed the lid, and carried it gingerly down the corridor to the dining hall.

"Merry Christmas, Mother." Lacy handed her the gift. "Please accept this humble gift. It's all I have left. But I love you so. I want you to have it in hopes that it will bring joy to sooth your aching heart."

With trembling hands, Queen Aikee opened the box and pulled out the once -shattered china doll. "She's lovely." The queen held the doll close then studied her cracked face. "She's more beautiful than ever … just like you, Lacy."

Lacy's lips quivered and tears moistened her cheeks. "I understand now, Mother. My heart had to be broken with compassion for the people, for Father, and for you before I could be transformed into the princess I need to be."

"You are a princess fair, my child and have filled my heart with more joy than you can imagine."

"I have changed. But still, Father has not returned nor have we received word of his safety or whereabouts."

"Not to worry, dear child." Mother's voice didn't sound convincing. "The kingdom flourishes with goodness since word has circulated about the princess's generosity. I'm sure—"

"Merry Christmas, my queen and my daughter." The king called as he swung open the door.

"Father!" Lacy rushed to his extended arms.

"My sweet princess." He embraced her. "'Tis so good to be home. I have much to tell you both about my adventures. But that will have to wait. Presently, I'm feeling especially generous. 'Tis Christmas, and the palace seems devoid of toys." He released his daughter with a kiss on the cheek. "What is your heart's desire? Name it, and I'll send for it at once."

Lacy smiled at him, turned to her mother who held the doll close to her chest, then looked up at her father. "You, Father, you are my Christmas wish."

Reflections

1. Christmas isn't over when the last gift is opened. The spirit of giving should be cultivated throughout the year.

2. Plan a post-Christmas visit to a nursing home or a shut-in. Take gifts if you want.

3. Remember your presence is far more important than presents. You might be someone's Christmas wish come true.

Prayer

Heavenly Father, use me to brighten people's lives throughout the coming year. In Jesus' name, amen.

ABOUT THE AUTHOR

Author/illustrator, BRENDA K. HENDRICKS, published three children's picture books: <u>What's the Buzz, Bumbly Bee?</u>, <u>What's Better than That, Seren Dippity?</u>, and <u>Much More to Christmas</u>. She also published a tween novel <u>Trouble at Camp Turnabout Creek</u>. Some of her short stories and devotions have been published in compilations, as well as in periodicals. She has also written children's short stories for Focus in the Family's *Club House Jr.* Her books are available on Amazon.

Brenda is the mother of two lovely grown daughters who have blessed her with seven grandchildren. She lives in a small town in Pennsylvania with her gracious (and good cook) husband and their slightly crazy Airedale.

Visit her blog at: BrendaKHendricks.com. Friend her on Facebook and Twitter. Visit her Etsy store, Creativity on the Loose, featuring her artwork.